MUHLENBERG

The Housing of the Poor in

American Cities.

THE

HOUSING OF THE POOR

IN

AMERICAN CITIES.

THE PRIZE ESSAY OF THE AMERICAN ECONOMIC
ASSOCIATION FOR 1892.

BY

MARCUS T. REYNOLDS, Ph. B., M. A.

McGrath Publishing Company
College Park, Maryland

Reprint McGrath Publishing Company 1969
Library of Congress Catalog Card Number: 79-100468

Manufactured in the United States of America
by Arno Press, Inc., New York

TABLE OF CONTENTS.

The Housing of the Poor.

I.

The Unsanitary Tenement—Origin, Growth and
Present Condition of the Tenement-
House System.

New York city offers the best example for the
study of the origin, growth and evil effects of the
tenement-house system in the New World. Not
only was it here that overcrowding first made itself
apparent, but the evil has grown here more rapidly
than elsewhere. Constantly receiving additions from
foreign ports, and recruiting its numbers from the
country, it is to-day the most densely settled city of
the world, while it is not rash to predict that long
before another century its population will surpass
that of London. The restricted limits of the city
will cause it to be always the most crowded town of
the continent, and therefore a more careful study of
this problem will be required here than in other cities,
more favorably situated. If the evils of the tenement are more striking in New York than elsewhere,
it has the honor of being far in advance of any other
city in respect of sanitary regulations, and has, indeed,
become a standard for other cities throughout the
country and in many of the European capitals.

The first effort to reform the tenement-house system in New York city was made in the winter of

1856-7, when a special committee was appointed by the legislature to examine and report upon the tenant-houses of the city. In its report this committee stated that, in its opinion, the causes of the tenant-house evil were over-population and destitution. Increasing traffic and manufacture had driven to the less thickly settled quarters of the city the wealthier citizens, whose spacious dwellings were then used as boarding-houses, or let in suites of apartments to the industrious poor who were employed in workshops, stores and warehouses in the vicinity. Rents were, at first, moderate, and the accommodations offered were suitable to the needs of their occupants; but a further pressure of population caused an increase of rent, and, at the same time, a decrease in the value obtained by it, as large suites of apartments were subdivided into small ones, large and light rooms partitioned into small and dark ones. The greater percentage of profit to be realized on such houses after their conversion into barracks, led to large purchases of property to be employed in the construction of others.

For more than five years no radical improvement was made in the tenant-houses, and meanwhile their evils continued to increase, until the public became thoroughly aroused as the system extended from ward to ward, the density of population increased, and it became evident that crime, debauchery and disease were becoming the habits of a large part of the population.

The Citizen's Association of New York was finally organized, and a Council of Hygiene and Public Health was appointed, which, early in 1864, made the first sanitary inspection of the tenement houses. In 1863

the discovery that in the city of New York the death
rate had increased from 1 in 46½ in 1810 to 1 in 35,
came like a shock to the citizens, which was not decreased by the plain statement of the case in the report of the Council of Hygiene and Public Health to
the Citizens' Association.

This stated that the evils of the system, due to for-
getfulness of the poor, and the absence of sanitary
regulation and advice, were constantly increasing.
Among such evils it enumerates filth, over-crowding,
lack of privacy and domesticity, lack of ventilation
and lighting, absence of supervision and of sanitary
regulation, a growing tendency to build to a greater
height in stories, to build more rear houses, back to
back with other buildings, to encroach further upon
courts and alleys, narrowing them into unventilated,
unlighted damp and well-like holes between the many-
storied front and rear tenements. The plans, construction and management of these houses had been left
almost exclusively to the caprice and selfishness
of men whose sole object had been to make small
investments and a borrowed capital pay enormous
advances, without regard to the tenants' welfare or
the public safety.

The condition of the houses of the poor is vividly
set forth in the report of the board of health, in 1866,
when the impending danger from cholera excited a
most thorough investigation of the sanitary condition of the city.

It was found that the first and at all times the most
prolific cause of disease was the insalubrious condition of most of the tenement-houses in the cities of
New York and Brooklyn. The provision of light and
ventilation was very insufficient, and the arrange-

ment of water-closets or privies could hardly be worse if actually intended to produce disease. The houses were almost invariably crowded, and ill-ventilated to such a degree as to render the air within them constantly impure and offensive. The drainage, of a very imperfect character, in many instances had no connection with the sewer, but consisted simply of surface gutters, by which all house-slops were conducted across the sidewalk and into the street. The privies were full and overflowing and generally very inadequate in number, there being frequently but one for the accommodation of from sixty to a hundred persons. Some of these were mere wells, extending from the upper floors to the cellars, and provided with an opening and a seat on each floor, but with no provision for water, and nothing to prevent the constant diffusion throughout the house of the emanations from the material accumulated below.

The basements were often below ground entirely, the ceiling being a foot or two below the level of the street, and were necessarily far more damp, dark and ill-ventilated than the remainder of the house. The cellars, when unoccupied, were frequently flooded to the depth of several inches with stagnant water, and were made the receptacles of garbage, excrement and refuse matter of every description. The halls and stairways were usually filthy and dark, the walls and banisters foul and damp, while the floors were not infrequently used as privies from lack of other provision. The dwelling-rooms were usually very inadequate in size for the accommodation of their occupants, and many of the sleeping-rooms were simply closets, without light or ventilation save by means of a single door. The yards were piled with garbage and filth.

In 1867 a census of the tenement-houses was taken with the following results: Total number, 18,582, of which 5,814 were in bad sanitary condition from neglect, 9,846 in bad sanitary condition from any cause, 2,922 in good condition. Thirty-two per cent. of the 52 per cent. in bad condition were in that state "purely from overflowing accumulation of filth, want of water supply and other results of neglect."

All this was twenty years ago. Twenty years of continual effort by the health department followed, and yet the report of the tenement commission of 1884 differs but little from that of 1864. The most important evils set forth by the chief inspector were found to be:

1. *Cellars.*—Broken drains and leaking pipes, saturating the soil and tainting the air of the whole house, the storage of rubbish, decaying fruit and vegetables are matters of constant occurrence, while the absence of faecal matter is the exception.

2. *Garbage.*—Where no provision is made for their removal, garbage, ashes, and refuse of all kinds are dumped into privies, yards, areas and light-shafts, or deposited on the roof, to be carried away by the wind.

3. *Light and Ventilation.*—Bedrooms may be said always to be dependent on the outer or living room for light and air. Even in cases where there are windows, they open into the halls, which are usually very dark, and entirely without ventilation.

4. *Light Shafts* are dangerous, as well as useless, as at present constructed, for the light is not available below the first or, at most, the second story from the roof. The shafts generally open into the cellar, in which case foul air is constantly being sucked into the various rooms. If the shaft is large enough to allow the light to strike the ground floor, it immediately becomes a receptacle for old clothes, food, and the like, and its usefulness as a light shaft ceases. When the shaft is not protected by a skylight, rags and rubbish of all kinds are thrown in, and it is sometimes used as a privy. In cases of fire the light shaft allows the flames to pass from floor to floor with great rapidity. The darkness of halls both by day and night is a serious matter, inducing as it does the gravest forms of immorality.

5. *Water Closets.*—In many cases privies, school sinks and water closets are found in the cellars, where there can be no ventilation, and the darkness hides the filth, which is constantly accumulating, while the foul odor rises through the house and taints the atmosphere to a noticeable degree. When the privies are located in the yard the distance from the upper floors is so great that tenants, and especially women, will not take the trouble to go so far. The normal condition of the privies in the yard being offensive, the more sensitive shrink from using them, and, in consequence, rooms, roofs and halls become foul, and the retention of decomposing matter in vessels in the rooms is of common occurrence.

The report of the Sanitary Aid Society in 1887 will appear exaggerated only to those who have never personally examined the worst dwellings of our poor. This description, however, would be an injustice to the *average* New York tenement:

"The investigation reveals a state of affairs, than which nothing more horrible can be imagined, and which, although perhaps equalled, can certainly not be surpassed in any European city. The condition of some houses is one of which no adequate conception can be formed without a personal visit. And let it be understood that the following facts are not selected cases or in any way exaggerated; they are absolutely true, and taken at random from among the many hundreds of instances. Indeed, the worst facts will not be given at all, for no respectable printer would print, and no daily paper admit, even the barest statement of the horrors and infamies that may be discovered by any one on a personal visit. To get into pestilential human rookeries you have to penetrate courts and alleys reeking with poisonous and malodorous gases, arising from accumulations of sewage and refuse scattered in all directions, and often flowing beneath your feet. You have to ascend rotten staircases, which threaten to give way beneath every step, and which in some places have already broken down, leaving gaps that imperil the limbs and lives of the unwary. You have to grope your way along dark and filthy passages swarming with vermin. Then, if you are not driven back by the intolerable stench, you may gain admittance to the dens in which thousands of human beings herd together. Walls and ceilings are black with the accretions of filth, which have gathered upon them through long years of neglect. It is exuding through cracks in the boards overhead; it is running down the walls; it is everywhere. What goes by the name of a window is half stuffed with rags or covered by boards to keep out wind and rain; the rest is so begrimed and obscured that scarcely any light can enter or anything be seen from the outside. Should you ascend to the attic, where at least some approach to fresh air might be expected from open or broken windows, you look out upon the roofs and ledges of lower tenements and discover that the sickly air which finds its way into the room has to pass over the putrefying carcases of dead cats or birds, or viler abomination still. The buildings are in such miserable repair as to suggest the thought that if the wind could only reach them they would soon be toppling about the heads of their occupants."

A typical tenement of 1863, selected as a good example of the buildings of those days, is here given. (See Fig. 1.)

Fig. 1.

This illustrates the floor plan of a multiple domicile constructed in 1863, designed for and occupied by twelve families on each flat. Situated on Broadway and another desirable street, near Central Park, this unventilated and fever-producing structure was filled to its utmost capacity with families who could pay well for rents and wished to live respectably. There are twelve living and twenty-one bed-rooms, and only six of the latter have any provision or possibility for the admission of light and air, excepting through the family sitting or living-room, being utterly dark, close and unventilated.

Nor is it in New York alone that the poor dwell in such wretched surroundings. In other cities, as may be seen from the reports of their respective aid societies, the situation is but little better.

This outline of the origin, growth and present condition of the tenement system in New York may be taken as a type of that in nearly all of the great cities of America.

In New York it was not long before the evil had assumed gigantic proportions. As early as December, 1864, according to the sanitary survey of the city, there were 15,309 tenements, which offered homes, such as they were, to 110,000 families, comprising in all 795,592 persons. Certain wards were crowded to the extent of 290,000 persons to the square mile, while in East London, which is its only rival, there were but 175,815 to the square mile.

Three years later the number had increased to 18,582 tenement-houses, of which but 2,922 were reported as in a good sanitary condition.

In 1883 an estimate showed that there were 18,996 tenements, containing 50 or more persons, while many harbored as many as 150. The population of the city was, in 1888, 1,526,081 persons, of which 1,093,701 were housed in the 32,390 tenements.

The report of the board of health for the year ending December 31, 1891, shows that there were, when the census was taken, in September of that year, 34,967 front tenements and 2,391 rear tenements. In these 276,565 families, numbering in all 1,225,411 persons, had their homes.

The following figures in regard to the proportion of persons and families to a dwelling are taken from the Extra Census Bulletin, No. 19, (April, 1892.)

Average number of persons to a dwelling[1] in	1850.	1880.	1890.
United States..........................	5 94	5.60	5.45
North Atlantic division	6.21	5.97	5.87
South Atlantic "	5.71	5 49	5.45
North Central "	5.83	5.47	5 22
South Central "	5.81	5.49	5 47
Western.............................	4.27	5 11	5.05

[1] A dwelling, for census purposes, means any building or place of abode in which any person was living at the time the census was taken.

2

Percentage of dwellings occupied (June 1890) by	1 to 10 persons.	More than 10 persons.	more than 20 persons.
United States (as a whole)............		4.35	
New York................	50.18	49.82	[1]28.83
Chicago.............................	75.46	24.54	
Philadelphia........................	95.61	4.39	

Percentage of population hiring dwellings having more than 10 occupants.		More than 20.
United States.......................	13.59	
New York....................	83.50	66.70
Chicago.............................	49.18	16 63
Philadelphia	12.79	3.41
Brooklyn...........	56 65	25.70
St. Louis	36 26	10.14
Boston.............................	47.80	13.93
Baltimore.........................	14 14	2.55
Cincinnati..........................	51.52	21.92
Buffalo.............................	30.02	
Newark.............................	40.01	10.25
Jersey City.........................	49.41	23.53
Providence.........................	37.76	7.49

Percentage of excess of families over dwellings in United States.	
1850.	7.02
1880.	11.06
1890.	10.51

[1]23,596 dwellings, of which 8,313 contain 21–30 persons.
        9,350   "   31–50   "
        5,460   "   51–100 "
          473   "   over 100 "

Cities.	Average Size of families.		Average number of persons to a dwelling.		Average number families to a dwelling.
	1880.	1890.	1880.	1890.	1890.
New York.....	4.96	4.84	16.37	18.52	3.82
Brooklyn......	4.92	4.72	9.11	9 80	2.08
Chicago........	5.19	4.99	8.24	8.60	1.72
Cincinnati.....	....	....	....	....	1.90
Boston.........	....	....	....	....	1.70
St. Louis.......	....	....	....	....	1.51
Baltimore......	....	....	....	....	1.20
Philadelphia ..	....	....	....	....	1.10

Cities.	Per Cent of Families in dwellings according to Specified number of Families.		
	1 family.	2 families.	3 families and over.
New York.....................	12.02	5.90	82.08
Chicago.....................	35.04	26.16	38.80
Philadelphia..................	84.64	10 46	4 90
Brooklyn	24.64	22.23	53 03
St. Louis....................	44.46	32 07	23.47
Boston......................	34.63	27.91	37.46
Baltimore....................	69.53	22 95	7.52
Cincinnati...................	31.96	19.55	48.49
San Francisco................	82.65	10.93	6 42
Cleveland....................	69.33	21.79	8 88
Buffalo......................	54.05	25.84	20.11
New Orleans..................	80 86	11.34	7.80
Pittsburg....................	69.14	22.44	8.42
Washington..................	78.75	15.79	5.46
Detroit......................	77.44	17.11	5.45
Milwaukee...........	62.67	26.90	10.43
Newark......................	35 22	30.80	33 98
Minneapolis..................	58.58	30.84	10 58
Jersey City..................	32.50	22.55	44.95
Louisville....................	60.30	21 61	18.09
Omaha.......................	81.97	12 69	5.34
Rochester....	78.76	14.33	6.91
St. Paul.....................	67 08	23.45	9 47
Kansas City..................	76.68	15.49	7.83
Providence...................	29.94	49.20	20.86
Denver	84.68	10.76	4.56
Indianapolis..................	86.16	8.72	5.12
Allegheny....................	62.70	28.04	9.26

Percentage of dwellings containing three families or more.	
New York..........	42.77
Brooklyn..........	25.60
Cincinnati.........	20.82
Chicago	17.09
St. Louis......	8.92
Boston.............	17.23
Newark	15.46
Jersey City.........	18.79
Baltimore	2.65
Philadelphia........	1.44

II.

Income and Expenses of the Working Classes.

It is not the purpose of this monograph to consider the general question of improving the condition of the poor, but to discuss one specific means for alleviating their sufferings, and for decreasing those evils which have their origin in, or are fostered by, the unsanitary tenement.

It is, however, pertinent to inquire how large a part the providing of comfortable and healthy homes plays in this more general question, and to consider what the situation of the poor would still be even if their homes were better.

The accommodations at the disposal of the working classes will always be dependent upon the amount of wages at their command. It is well, therefore, to know what this sum is, and what proportion of it may be expended upon rent. The following tables are taken from the sixteenth annual report of the Massachusetts Bureau of Statistics of Labor, entitled "Comparative Wages, Prices and Cost of Living."

Let us first consider the general average weekly wages paid to all employees in the various industries, which have been broadly classified under six heads.

Textiles.................................... $6 91
Clothing................................... 10 88
Building................................... 12 67
Metallic Work.............................. 11 26
Wood Work................................. 12 34
Other Industries........................... 11 59

If we then examine the average weekly wages of those employed in all industries and the ratio in which the wages of the women and children stand to those of the men, we shall be able to learn what amount of money is at the disposal of a family of any given size. These averages are found to be as follows:

Average *highest* weekly wages paid to men........$25 41
     "   "   "   "   "   women....... 8 57
     "   "   "   "   "   young persons 6 94
     "   "   "   "   "   children...... 4 64

Average *lowest* weekly wages paid to men......... $7 09
     "   "   "   "   "   women....... 4 62
     "   "   "   "   "   young persons 4 26
     "   "   "   "   "   children...... 3 09

Average weekly wages paid to men.............. $11 85
     "   "   "   "   women............. 6 09
     "   "   "   "   young persons...... 5 10
     "   "   "   "   children........... 3 81

General Average weekly wages paid to employees working by
     the *day*...$10 46
General Average weekly wages paid to employees working by
     the *piece*.. 9 85
General Average weekly wages paid to employees working by
     the *day* or *piece*....................................... 9 69
General Average weekly wages paid to *all employees*......... 10 32
Percentage of employees receiving *more than* the general aver-
     age weekly wage..47.5%
Percentage of employees receiving less than the general aver-
     age weekly wages...52.5%

By comparing the general average weekly wages paid to men, women, young persons and children, we may discover the ratio of wages of the women, young persons and children to those of the men. Taking the latter as the basis of comparison the ratio of wages paid to women is as 51.39 to 100; those paid to young persons as 43.04 to 100; and those paid to children as 32.15 to 100.

In 1885 the Bureau of Statistics of Labor secured nineteen budgets or accounts of annual expenditure. The results are given in the following table:

WORKINGMEN'S BUDGETS.

No.	Persons in Family.			At Work.			Earnings of head of Family.	Earnings of Members of Family.	Total Earnings.	Total Expenses.	Surplus or Debt.
	Adults.	Child-ren.	Total.	Adults	Child-ren.	Total.					
1	2	4	6	1	1	2	$616	$224	$840	$661	+179
2	2	4	6	1	2	3	572	364	936	936	.....
3	2	2	4	1	..	1	616	....	616	649	33
4	3	3	6	1	2	3	624	390	1014	1014	.....
5	2	4	6	2	..	2	450	156	606	432	+174
6	2	5	7	1	2	3	390	456	846	846	.....
7	2	4	6	1	2	3	385	358	743	743	.....
8	3	3	6	1	2	3	416	195	611	611	.....
9	2	4	6	1	1	2	520	184	704	653	+ 51
10	2	4	6	1	2	3	618	282	890	890	.....
11	2	4	6	1	1	2	624	300	924	924	....
12	3	..	3	2	..	2	520	780	1300	1185	+115
13	2	3	5	1	1	2	614	260	874	874	.....
14	2	1	3	1	..	1	1040	....	1040	834	+206
15	2	..	2	2	..	2	520	260	780	540	+240
16	2	4	6	1	1	2	494	156	650	650	.....
17	2	2	4	1	1	2	470	156	626	626	.....
18	2	3	5	1	1	2	520	130	650	650	.....
19	2	4	6	1	..	1	616	....	616	616	.....

Averaging these nineteen budgets, we obtain the following results:

Classification.	Average.	Per cent.
Persons in family...............................	5.21	.....
Adults..	2.16	41.26
Children.....................................	3.05	58.54
Number at work...............................	2.16	.....
Adults..	1.16	53.70
Children.....................................	1.00	46.30
Total earnings..........	$803.47	.....
Earnings of head of family	558.68	69.53
Earnings of members of family..............	244.79	30.47
Total expenses...............................	754.42	93.89
Surplus......................................	49.05	6.11

It must be noticed how nearly the expenditures reach the amount of wages at the disposal of the average family. Forty-nine dollars is a small margin with which to meet any emergency, and we realize that in whatever way the poor are to be provided with better homes, it cannot be done by offering accommodations at higher prices. Better value must be given for the amount now expended for rent.

The items which make up the total expense column of these nineteen budgets are given in the following table:

No.	Total expenses.	Rent.	Subsistence.	Fuel.	Clothing.	Sundries.
1	$661	$144	$265	$40	$102	$110
2	936	192	460	40	215	29
3	649	Owned.	409	40	100	100
4	1,014	240	520	40	155	59
5	432	72	300	..	40	20
6	846	150	430	30	142	94
7	743	96	360	30	140	117
8	611	144	325	30	80	32
9	653	66	325	..	150	112
10	890	168	471	40	154	57
11	924	180	511	40	116	77
12	1,185	400	325	80	190	190
13	874	150	385	40	95	204
14	834	168	405	40	150	71
15	540	156	352	15	68	49
16	650	120	345	20	105	60
17	626	96	320	25	85	100
18	650	144	350	26	100	30
19	616	144	305	40	100	27

We have already seen that the average expenses per family amounted to $754.42. Averaging the above table we find that this expense is distributed under the several heads in the following proportion:

Classification.	Average.	Per cent.
Rent...	$148.95	19.74
Subsistence......	371.73	49.28
Fuel..	32.42	4.30
Clothing...	120.37	15.95
Sundries...	80.95	10.73
	$754.42	100

The proportional parts of a workingman's income required for clothing, rent, provisions, etc., was first arrived at and propounded as an economic law by Dr. Engel, chief of the Royal Prussian Bureau of Statistics, at Berlin.

The following table gives the facts upon which Dr. Engel bases the propositions given below:

Items of expenditure.	Percentage of the expenditure of the family of a working man with an income of		
	$225–$300 Per cent.	$450–$600 Per cent.	$750–$1,100 Per cent.
Subsistence.......................	62 ⎫	55 ⎫	50 ⎫
Clothing	16 ⎬ 95	18 ⎬ 90	18 ⎬ 85
Lodging..........................	12 ⎪	12 ⎪	12 ⎪
Fire and lighting.................	5 ⎭	5 ⎭	5 ⎭
Education, public worship, etc......	2 ⎫	3.5 ⎫	5.5 ⎫
Legal protection..................	1 ⎬ 5	2. ⎬ 10	3. ⎬ 15
Care of health....................	1 ⎪	2. ⎪	3. ⎪
Comfort, mental and bodily health..	1 ⎭	1.5 ⎭	3.5 ⎭

The propositions arrived at from the foregoing figures are:

First.—The greater the income the smaller the relative percentage of outlay for subsistence.

Second.—The percentage of outlay for clothing is approximately the same, whatever the income.

Third.—The percentage of outlay for lodging or rent and for fuel and light is invariably the same, whatever the income.

Fourth.—As the income increases in amount, the percentage of outlay for sundries becomes greater.

The following table shows the comparative percentages of expenditures in the United States and in Europe:

Items of Expenditure.	United States. Per cent.	Europe. Per cent.
Subsistence	45.33	53.18
Clothing..............................	18.47	18.06
Rent.................................	18.58	12.74
Fuel.................................	4.97	4.25
Sundries.............................	12.65	11.77
Totals...............................	100.00	100.00

The Massachusetts Bureau of Statistics of Labor in its sixth annual report gives an interesting table showing the percentages of expenditure of workingmen's families, with incomes ranging from $300 to $1,200.

It is reprinted here, and the percentages have been expressed in dollars that the amounts expended for various items may be seen the better:

Items of expenditure.	$300 to $450 Per cent.	Average. $375	$450 to $600 Per cent.	Average. $525	$600 to $750 Per cent.	Average. $675	$750 to $1,200 Per cent.	Average. $975	Above $1,200. Per cent.	$12.00
Subsistence.	64	$240.00	63	$330.75	60	$405.00	56	$546.00	51	$612
Clothing.....	7	26 25	10.5	55.12	14	94.50	15	146.25	19	228
Rent.........	20 \}97	75.00	15.5 \}95	81.38	14 \}94	94.50	17 \}94	165.75	15 \}90	180
Fuel	6	22.50	6	31.50	6	40.50	6	58.50	5	60
Sundries.....	3.3	11.25	5 5	26.25	6 6	40.50	6 6	58.50	10 10	120
Totals........	100	$375.00	100	$525 00	100	$5.5.00	100	$975.00	10ე	$1,200

Expenditure of the family of a workingman with an income of

Comparing these results with the propositions laid down by Dr. Engel, we find that the greater the income the smaller is the relative percentage of outlay for subsistence. The greater the income the greater is the relative outlay for clothing, the percentage of which increases constantly and greatly. The percentage expended for rent, so far from remaining "invariably the same," fluctuates in a remarkable degree. Statistics gathered from many states confirm the general truth of Engel's law. Unfortunately this matter has not received attention from the census bureau.

Having examined the amount of income at the disposal of the workingman and the percentage which he devotes to the payment of rent, we will now consider the prices paid for board and lodging, taking again the state of Massachusetts in illustration.

The bureau of labor statistics found, after compiling a large number of budgets, that the average rent of *one room* was 66 cents per week, $2.86 per month, or $34.38 per year. The average rent for various sized tenements can be easily computed on that basis.

The average price of board and lodging for men was $4.79 per week, for women $3.19 per week; for men per month $20.76, for women $13,82; for men per year $249.08, for women $165.88.

For board without lodging the average rates for men per week were $3.84; for women $2.56; per month, men $16.68, women, $11.09; per year, men $199.68, women $133.12.

For lodging by itself the average rates per week for men were $2.20, for women $1.46; per month, for men \$9.53, for women \$6.33; per year, for men \$114.40, and for women \$75.92.

In this monograph some attention is paid to the various ways in which the poor are housed in England. It is well, before considering these methods, to know the prices paid for rent in that country. For purposes of comparison these figures are given, together with those presented above, in the following table:

	Massachusetts.			England.		
	Weekly.	Monthly.	Yearly.	Weekly.	Monthly.	Yearly.
Rent of one room..	\$ .66	\$2.86	\$34.38	\$ .35	\$1 51	\$18.02
Board & Men..... Lodging Women.	\$4 79 3.19	\$20.76 13.82	\$249.08 165.88	\$3.37 2.37	\$14.58 10.28	\$174.98 123 91
Board Men..... alone. Women.	\$3.84 2.56	\$16.68 11.09	\$199 68 133.12	\$2 34 1.56	\$10.18 6 79	\$121.00 81.22
Lodging Men..... alone. Women.	\$2.20 1 46	\$ 9.53 6.33	\$114.40 75.92	\$1.34 .86	\$ 5.81 3.85	\$ 69 78 46.27

It may be seen that rents are 89.62 per cent. higher, and board and lodging 39.01 per cent. higher in Massachusetts than in England.

We have seen that in the United States 45 per cent. of the income of the workingman is expended for subsistence, and only 18 per cent. for rent. The question might then naturally be asked, why, since so small a proportion is paid for rent, do we pay so much more attention to the housing of the poor than to bettering their condition by making this expenditure for subsistence of more service by offering them facilities for obtaining the same quality and quantity of food at a lower rate?

The answer is that the relative importance of good homes and good food cannot be measured by that of cheap homes and cheap food. That is, if a man, who had barely enough income to supply himself with a fair room and fair food, should become possessed of greater resources, he could better expend them in increasing the comforts of his home than in bettering the quality or quantity of his food. Unsanitary homes injure their occupants both physically and morally; plain food injures a person but slightly, if at all. The great difference in the outlay for subsistence and for rent suggests that the poor may be greatly benefited by a wiser expenditure on their homes. While this monograph does not deal with the improvement of the condition of the poor, this subject receives some attention in a later chapter, and some suggestions are offered for the establishment of what I christen, for lack of a better term, the "boarding tenement."

The importance of sanitary homes for the poor can best be emphasized by considering from an economic standpoint the mischiefs which have their birth in the unsanitary tenement, or, having their origin elsewhere, find here a congenial soil for their development into such evils as threaten the mental, moral and physical health of the individual, and even that of the community at large.

III.

Importance of Reform—Causes of Over-Crowding—Evils of Over-Crowded Tenements.

Too much attention has been paid to the personal and merely bodily discomforts of the occupants of our unsanitary tenements, while the far-reaching and more deadly evils, which have their origin here, are lost sight of in the lengthy descriptions of the want and suffering of the unfortunate poor.

Descriptions of specific cases have, therefore, been omitted here purposely, as they have been fully dwelt on by those who have made it their life work to labor among the poor, and who have sketched the horrors of tenement life in the strongest and darkest colors. A score of such books and reports of various charitable organizations are given in the bibliography. It would seem to be more profitable, therefore, to examine into the evils which are inseparably connected with the tenement-house system, which affect the wealth, morality and the very being of the nation—evils from whose pernicious influence no one, no matter what his position, is entirely safe, and which it is the interest of all to lessen in every way possible.

The overcrowding which is at the root of all these evils is due to many causes. Prominent among them are the fascination which a large town exercises over the dwellers in the country; the opportunities offered the poor and lazy to dwell at the expense of the rich, and the greater demand for labor. Indeed, as Lord Salisbury says, "the evil is directly caused by prosperity; as competition for work becomes closer the suffering of the poor from bad housing becomes more severe." But whatever the causes of the over-crowded tenement may be, the evils which accompany it are many and terrible. I have made an attempt to tabulate them, but the task is a most difficult one, so inseparably connnected in cause and effect are many of them. The more important of the resulting evils will now be briefly considered.

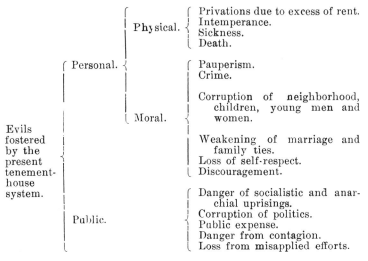

Evils fostered by the present tenement-house system.

Personal.

Physical. — Privations due to excess of rent. Intemperance. Sickness. Death.

Moral. — Pauperism. Crime.

Corruption of neighborhood, children, young men and women.

Weakening of marriage and family ties. Loss of self-respect. Discouragement.

Public. — Danger of socialistic and anar-chial uprisings. Corruption of politics. Public expense. Danger from contagion. Loss from misapplied efforts.

Privations Due to the Excess of Rent.—The exorbitant rent charged the very poor is the immediate source of much suffering, and too often of crime.

Over-crowding is made possible by the fact that the demand far exceeds the supply. A workman can live outside the city, but he is seldom willing to prolong the labor of the day by the hour or more which must be spent in reaching his place of employment in the morning and in returning to his home at night.

Many persons, who have been tenement lodgers, but who have in some way acquired a little capital, know how profitable this investment is and build tenements themselves. Their capital is small and the buildings are erected at the smallest expense. They know, also, that every room which is situated near the centres of employment is eagerly competed for, and that they are sure of tenants, no matter how wretched the rooms may be. Repairs and improvements are, therefore, seldom if ever made.

A few examples will show how excessive the rent is in many instances. In Bedford street, Philadelphia, a rookery worth $500 brought $80 a month. In New York the owner of a building destroyed by fire stated himself that it was fully insured for $800, though it brought him in $600 a year rent. Forty per cent. was declared by witnesses before a senate committee to be a fair average interest on tenement property. Instances were given of rates of interest being one hundred per cent. and over. The following are a few typical examples of the rents of tenements in New York: One room and dark alcove, $10 per month; one room and dark alcove (a little larger), $12.25; one room and two dark alcoves, $12.50; one parlor, two bed-rooms and kitchen, $22.

Rents will continue to be excessive until there are offered the working classes enough cheap and healthy homes to supply the demand. Then no longer will they be forced to content themselves with whatever wretched places are offered, and to pay exorbitant prices.

Admitting that the rents charged are excessive, let us see what evils result therefrom. To do this it is necessary only to examine the ways in which the rent is met. The usual means is by taking boarders or lodgers; for these no larger accommodations are taken, and the new-comers share the room or rooms, none too large for the original family.

Many instances have been discovered where a family occupying a single room has taken, as boarders, not one other family but several. The debasing effect upon any family life which might otherwise exist is too obvious to need discussion.

It is a frequent practice to let the rooms by day to the men and women who busy themselves with making "tenement-made" clothing. The only limit to the number of persons thus accommodated is the seating capacity of the room. The demands of ventilation are disregarded, and the air, which was fetid in the morning from the nightly exhalations of its occupants, becomes saturated with germs from the unclean and often diseased bodies of the "sweaters" who breathe it again and again. This is continued day after day, until the room and all its contents reek with the accretions of filth accumulated during an indefinite period. The clothing made in these places is afterward exposed for sale in all parts of the city, and, when worn, meets us at every corner. In an atmosphere such as this, family ties and human life cannot exist. Still another way of making others pay the rent is the letting of the room by night for immoral purposes.

The excess of rent is also met by a proportional decrease in the purchase of fuel, food, clothing and other necessaries, and even then the family can often afford but a single room, whose evil influences are studied in a later portion of this article.

Intemperance.—It is a self-evident fact that unpleasant surroundings and intemperance are as closely allied as the sequence of cause and effect can bind them. A silent acknowledgment is the comfort with which a saloon in the slums is fitted up, the proprietor knowing well what bait will prove most attractive to his customers.

It is quite true that in many a tenement block the saloon is the one bright, cheerful place to be found, and it would be strange if the workman, returning tired from his day's labor, did not prefer the warm and comfortable saloon to the cold and cheerless place, which he calls his home. Writers on temperance, in both Europe and America, have reached the conclusion that the re-housing of the poor would be a substantial aid to their cause.

A legislative committee in New York, appointed to investigate the question, recommended "the prevention of drunkenness by providing every man a clean and comfortable home." The futility of all attempts to benefit labor before this remedy has been applied is affirmed by a writer in the *Fortnightly Review,* who thus disposes of the question: "It is useless to increase wages and to lessen the hours of labor, so long as the workman is compelled to live in the pesthouses we have described; nay, it is worse than useless, as extra wages and leisure operate as incentives to drunkenness."

Too great emphasis cannot be given to the fact that the saloon is merely the expression of the unconscious desire, prevalent in most men, for the comfort to body and mind offered by a warm, comfortably furnished and well lighted room. It is not the liquor which gives the saloon its chief attraction, but the

3

companionship found there. As long as this is only offered in drinking places, just so long will the saloons be well patronized. As soon as the home means something more to the working man than a place in which he eats and sleeps, just so soon will the saloon lose its chief attraction for him.

Sickness and Mortality.—Of all the evils which are due to the tenement-house system, the one that concerns the public most directly is the danger, which at all times threatens the community, from the presence in the tenement district of contagious and infectious diseases.

That thousands of dwellings in all of our cities are in a more or less unsanitary condition, while their occupants lead lives conducive to the birth of disease, is too well known to need more than the mention.

The working people, who spend the night in such dirty and disease-breeding places, disperse in the morning, and by the nature of their occupations, find their way to all portions of the city, and are thrown in contact with all classes of society. It is not too much to say that there is not a home which is not entered daily by at least one person, who has his home in a dwelling occupied exclusively by the working classes.

Much of the clothing offered for sale by the best dry-good stores and tailors has passed through the hands of like persons, while no small portion has been made in their dwellings. Clothes sent out to be washed are usually carried to the homes of the working people.

Though we might prevent the actual entrance into our homes of persons carrying about with them the germs of disease, it is quite impossible to prevent contact in the street, or elsewhere, with such persons.

I do not wish to be understood as stating that all dwellings of the working classes are in a more or less unsanitary condition, or that all dirty and un-healthy dwellings are of necessity dangerous to the health of the community. The number of dwellings in an unsanitary condition is, however, very large, as the reports of various boards of health will testify, and even in buildings which are for the most part clean and in good condition, there usually exist one or more rooms, the tenants of which persist in keep-ing them in a filthy condition. While these places may not all produce contagious or infectious germs, there is a great probability that many of them do, while all are well fitted to harbor any disease which may present itself. In times of epidemics, if the disease obtains a foot-hold in the tenement-house district, it is almost impossible to overpower it, until it has burnt itself out. In Gotham Court, New York city, the mortality in the last great cholera epidemic reached the height of 195 in 1,000 inhabitants. Here it was that a sanitary inspector counted 146 cases of sick-ness, including all kinds of infectious diseases, from small-pox down. Of 138 children born in three years only 61 lived. In the old Baptist church not far away, the rear half of which had been divided into tenements, the annual death rate was 75 in 1,000. In the Bend the mortality in 1882 was 68.28; that of Mulberry street, in 1888 was 38.05.

The hand of disease and death falls most heavily on the children. The death rate for them reached in Baxter street 146.02; in Mulberry street 136.70.

Possibly the full importance of these figures can be appreciated only by comparing them with the mortality of various cities at nearly the same time:

```
Death rate in New York, 1889............. 25.19
    "        "    Boston,      "   ............. 24.42
    "        "    Brooklyn,    "   ............. 22.5
    "        "    Philadelphia,"   ............. 19.7
    "        "    London,      "   ............. 17.4
```

The sanitary police of New York city took, in 1888, a census of the tenement-house population, to which the registrar of vital statistics draws attention in a preliminary report on the death rates of the city. Some unexpected conclusions are reached. With a total tenement-house population of 1,117,257 and 29,172 deaths, we have a death rate for the year of 26.11 per 1,000 living, as against a general death rate for the city of 26.33. The death rate of the tenement-house population is thus seen to be lower than that of the remaining population of the city.

The death rate of persons five years of age and over decreases with increase in number of tenants, while the death rate of children under five years increases, until there are more than eighty tenants to a house after which it decreases. The probable reason for the progressive decrease of death rate is that the tenants of the larger houses live under better sanitary conditions than those of the smaller, with the exception of density of population. These better sanitary conditions are largely owing to the greater facility of inspection and superintendence in the larger houses. As regards special diseases, it was found that while diarrhœal diseases and diphtheria show a greater death rate in the larger houses, phthisis and pneumonia show comparatively little

difference, that little being in favor of the larger
houses. It may be noted, as a possible partial explanation of the lesser death rate of the poorer classes,
that they pass much of their lives out of doors, and
when in-doors live in rooms without carpets or
papered walls to catch and propagate micro-organ-
isms, with bare floors that are washed frequently.

A comparison of the vital statistics of 1888 with
those of 1869 shows that this disproportion has not
always existed:

Year.	General Death-rate.	Tenement Death-rate.
1869.	28.13	28.35
1888.	26.33	22.71

The report of the board of health for 1891 shows
the same remarkable fact presented in 1888, that the
death rate is the highest in the houses which contain the fewest occupants. This report finds that
the highest death rates for the thickly populated districts are in districts largely inhabited by Italians,
and the lowest in the poor Jewish district. As regards particular diseases, the death rates from bron-
chitis, diarrhœal diseases, diphtheria and croup,
measles, pneumonia and scarlet fever increase, while
Brights' disease, heart diseases, influenza, malarial
fevers, phthisis and typhoid fever decrease as the
number of tenants increases. The report gives as a
probable reason for the progressively decreasing
death rate, more frequent removal to hospitals from
the larger houses, adducing the above figures of
special diseases to show decreasing death rate in
such diseases as would be more likely to be removed
to the hospitals.

The public dispensaries of New York alone annually provide medical aid for 1,500,000 persons, nearly all of whom are inhabitants of tenement districts. Healthy homes save twenty days of idleness yearly through sickness for every inhabitant, according to the estimate of an officer of the London board of health.

The public loss in money is enormous; the poor alone understand the full meaning of the individual loss of wages and money. But the greater evil is the danger to the community from disease. This may, perhaps, be the means, where all others have failed, of doing away with the most crying evils of the tenement, for it is self-interest which enforces the dictates of humanity.

Pauperism.—Pauperism may be considered as one of the contagious diseases common to the tenement-house system. Many instances might be cited of houses which at one time were occupied by hard-working persons, but which, by the contagious presence of one person, too lazy or too vicious to work, had become filled almost exclusively with paupers. More than a hundred and twenty paupers have been reported as living in a single tenement.

In a time of temporary embarrassment many persons, hitherto wage-earners, seek relief by appealing to the charity of others; then, finding it an easy matter to obtain a sufficient amount for support, all desire for earning wages is lost, and henceforth they become paupers.

Others in the same tenement, seeing how easy it is to obtain in a few hours without labor more money than they can earn by a day's hard work, soon follow their example.

This is not to be wondered at. The poor are not particularly endowed with moral courage, and are as anxious as the rest of the world to obtain the greatest returns for the least expenditure of labor.

There is no accurate estimate of the number of paupers in the United States. Mr. Charles D. Kellogg, secretary of the New York Charity Organization Society, has estimated that 3,000,000 were wholly or partially supported by alms during a single year, while the *State's Charities Record* reports 500,000 paupers in New York state as almsmen of the state.

Perhaps the figures which carry the greatest meaning are the number of pauper burials, which represent only the poorest of the poor. For the five years ending 1888 over 10 per cent of all the burials in New York city were in the potter's field, and this despite the fact that the poor have in most cases elaborate funerals, while many are provided by the numerous aid societies.

Professor Richard T. Ely, in an article investigating the causes of pauperism in the United States, reached the conclusion that "the most general statement possible is that the causes of poverty are heredity and environment, producing weak physical, mental and moral constitutions."

The influences of tenement life were also recognized by Dugdale, who, in his sociological study, "The Jukes," says: "The logical induction seems to be that environment is the ultimate controlling factor in determining careers, placing heredity itself as an organized result of invariable environments."[1]

---

[1] "Pauperism in the United States," *North American Review*, April, 1891.

Tenement-house reform has long been recognized as the key to the problem of pauperism in the city. We can never get rid of the tenement-house system or of pauperism, but by the reform of the former we shall accomplish more towards exterminating the latter than by any other means that has yet been suggested.

Crime.—The legislative committee appointed in 1885 to investigate the causes of the increase of crime in New York state reached the conclusion that it was largely due to the evil influences of the tenement upon the young. The following extract, from the testimony of Dr. Elisha Harris, corresponding secretary of the Prison Association of New York, before that committee, clearly shows the connection between crime and the tenement:

"The younger criminals seem to come almost exclusively from the worst tenement-house districts. When the great riot occurred in 1863 every hiding place and nursery of crime discovered itself by immediate and active participation in the operations of the mob. Those very places and domiciles, and all that are like them, are to-day nurseries of crime, and of the vices and disorderly courses which lead to crime. By far the largest part—eighty per cent. at least—of the crimes against property and against the person are perpetrated by individuals who have either lost connection with home life, or never had any, or whose homes had ceased to be sufficiently separate, decent and desirable to afford what are regarded as ordinary wholesome influences of home and family."

In the *North American Review* of September, 1889, Superintendent Byrnes calls attention to the reformation of the tenement-house system as the most efficient method of reducing the number of our criminals. In this article, entitled "Nurseries of Crime," he emphatically states that the direct causes of many an honest man's fall are the absence of all home life and the consequent corrupting acquaintance of the young with the criminal classes.

The best proof of the intimate connection between crime and the loss of home influences is the fact that in many towns where a wide-reaching reform of the tenement-house system has taken place, the number of crimes committed during a given period has greatly fallen off. Glasgow is a striking example of this. Here the number of crimes fell from 10,899 in 1867 to 7,869 in 1873. This decrease is undoubtedly due to the extensive reforms effected in that city, by the appropriation and rebuilding of large districts.

In connection with this subject, it is well to point out the evils which the present system of cheap lodging-houses is responsible for. In such places congregate the stranger to the city, the honest-man-out-of-work, and the criminal.

The criminal and the easy method of obtaining a living at the expense of others, which he personifies, are thus brought to the notice of the other two classes. These persons, from the nature of their circumstances, are in danger of losing what moral courage they may possess, by the undermining influence of the absence of all home ties, of a desire for excitement and of actual want. From these classes the ranks of the criminals are constantly recruited, and many of them can look back upon the cheap lodging-house as the place where first the temptation was presented that caused their subsequent downfall.

Evil Influences.—One of the curses of the tenement system is the leveling influence which the worst houses exercise upon all the others. Overcrowd-

ing results in the inevitable association of honest
people with criminals.   The effect of this association
is especially bad for the young of both sexes.   The
boys' ideal hero is the clever thief or the successful
burglar; the girls admire and envy the woman of evil
life, who obtains such pleasures and comforts as they
are capable of appreciating, at such an easy cost.
The marriage tie also is weakened.   As the conditions
of life become too hard, the man is tempted to desert
his family, either alone or with another companion.

If, as Cardinal Manning says, domestic life creates
a people, it is pertinent to ask ourselves, what sort
of people the domestic life of our tenements will
produce us.   We may indeed inquire if there is any
domestic life possible in our tenements as constituted
to-day.   The home life of a family, in which both
parents drink and are mutually unfaithful, whose
sons belong perhaps to the "gangs" of our streets,
and whose girls seek a livelihood upon the pavement,
can not be productive of good.   A family which lets
the room by day to the "sweaters," by night for immoral purposes, can hardly be of a kind to produce a
very high grade of citizenship.   Nor can the domestic life found in a "room 12x12, with five families
living in it, comprising twenty persons of both sexes
and all ages, with only two beds, without partition,
screen, chair or table," have a beneficial effect upon
the characters of the younger members.

Habitual contact with uncleanliness lowers self-
respect.   Bishop Potter has said: "The connection
between dirt and degradation is more intimate than
most people are willing to recognize.   No one, who
has known any other condition, can be subjected to
conditions of life in which cleanliness is practically

impossible, whether of body or raiment, without a steady and sure deterioration of the whole moral tone."

Not the least evil of the overcrowded tenement is the depression of body and mind which they create, and which is an almost insuperable obstacle to the action of any elevating or refining agencies.

Public Dangers.—While the public is indirectly affected by the misfortunes of its component parts, it is also directly affected in more than one way by the over-crowded tenement. One danger, which grows more and more apparent every year, is the danger of a social revolution. What manner of men and women must these millions of paupers be, if they can see without resentment the complacent exhibition of opulence and ease, which is forever flaunted in their faces, within a few hundred yards of the noisome courts and alleys. The cry of distress is as yet almost inarticulate, but it will not always remain so. It would be strange, indeed, if the striking contrast between the luxury of the rich and the misery of the poor, jostling one another upon every street corner, did not provoke bitter remonstrance, and even active revolt, on the part of the less fortunate members of our body politic.

The wide circulation of such a book as " Progress and Poverty," and the acceptance which the suggestions it contains have found among the working classes, are full of significance and warning.

The wanton display of riches and the unhappiness of the poor were little greater in France in 1789 than they are in America a century later, and while there is little present danger that similar results will follow, it is well to keep in mind that saying of Danton: "If you suffer the poor to grow up as animals, they may chance to become beasts and rend you."

The public seems able to bear with equanimity the story of the misfortunes of the poor; it only shudders when the danger from contagion is hinted at; but it might arouse itself if a revolution were threatened, for "when property becomes alarmed, the outcry which it makes is deafening."

The influence on politics is powerful for evil. Indifference to the conditions of the tenement house will always show itself in the corruption of public affairs. An instance of this is furnished by New York under the rule of Tweed, himself of tenement origin, when the administration of public affairs was notoriously corrupt, and the tenements in their worst condition. With the improvement of one went the reform of the other.

It is needless to point out the great public expense from the sickness and death, crime and pauperism, engendered in the tenement. The yearly loss from wasted efforts due to the same must not be lost sight of.

We have sketched the history of the tenement system, have compared a typical tenement of thirty years ago with the *unsanitary* tenement of to-day, and have outlined the chief evils which seem inseparably connected with them.

We will now examine the various ways in which homes of the poor may be improved. These have been here classed under five heads—

1. Legislation.
2. Improvement of existing buildings.
3. Erection of better single tenements.

4. Erection of "model tenements."

5. Erection of cottages in the suburbs.

The advantages and disadvantages of each method will be discussed, examples of the most successful results will be given, and the benefits that each have accomplished will be considered by a comparison of the percentage of births, sickness, mortality and crime of certain buildings or localities, with those in which no attempt at reform has been made.

IV.

Efforts to Improve the Homes of the Poor by Legislation.

Many have seen in legislation a sure and easy solution of our problem. It can take two forms: first, that of expropriation of districts which are beyond reform; and, second, a compulsion to repair and keep in order unsanitary buildings, and legal restrictions on the building of tenements.

Expropriation has been extensively tried in England, Scotland, and in many of the cities of the continent, particularly in Paris, with more or less success. The justness of trying the same method, even in America, cannot be questioned. The principle of "*Salus populi suprema lex*" is an old and undisputed one. Its supporters contend that the state has too long made itself the champion of the individual; that it should rather assert the rights of the many.

The object of expropriation and the regulations which should control it have thus been outlined: The local authority should be empowered to reconstruct such areas as are found to be in such a condition as to be injurious to the moral and physical welfare of the people and to be unfit for habitation and injurious to the surrounding population. The recommendation has been made that—

1. The municipality should be compelled to make the improvements declared necessary by the municipal medical officers of health or by the medical officer appointed by the government for that purpose.

2. The municipality should have the right of compulsory purchase.

3. The price should be determined by a governmental valuation and should never exceed ten years purchase of the actual rental.

4. The cost incurred should be defrayed by a tax levied upon the owners of property within the district where the improvement is to be made, in proportion to the value of the buildings to such property.

Under the powers conferred upon the Metropolitan Board of Works by the acts of 1875 and 1879, 42 acres, inhabited by 20,335 persons, in the city of London, were cleared of the unsanitary buildings which covered them. The net loss was estimated at £1,211,-336, or about £60 per head of the population assumed to be benefited. The cost of the land was 17 *s.* per square foot. The price obtained, when sold with the obligation to build workingmen's dwellings, was 3 *s.* 4 *d.* per foot. The value for commercial purposes was 10 *s.* per square foot. Thus the owners made a profit of 7 *s.* per square foot on the ordinary market value of their land, and 13 *s.* more than their land was worth for the purpose for which they had been employing it. As a result, many persons bought property and were glad to see it fall into as unsanitary a state as possible, that they might sell it at an artificial price. A premium was thus placed upon neglect and willful indifference to sanitary provisions.

The Corporation of London bought 111,000 square feet at 43 *s.* per foot, the value of which for commercial purposes was 34 *s.* per square foot. In this instance the owners received 9 *s.* more than they could have obtained in open market, and 37 *s.* more than the land was worth for workmen's dwellings. The cost to the tax-payers was £270,000, or £120 per head for the people displaced. In Liverpool 20,720 square yards were purchased for £67,000. The results reached were very unsatisfactory and the project was finally abandoned.

The town council of Edinburgh dispossessed, under the act of 1867, 1,500 families, at a cost of £3,505,000.

The city of Glasgow may serve as an excellent example of expropriation, not only because of the large scale on which the work was undertaken, but because of the shrewdness with which it was carried out and the good results that followed. The city is very old, and, like all mediæval towns, densely built. The lines of the streets in the older parts of the town had not been disturbed, though the buildings had been rebuilt, so that in certain portions it was more densely crowded than any European town. The city was a maze of narrow and filthy streets, with lanes and alleys lined with old decaying houses, in which swarmed a population so dense that in some cases it reached a thousand to the acre.

In 1866 a plan was devised for redeeming a tract of eighty-eight acres, comprising the whole of the ancient town. Authority was obtained from Parliament to purchase property and tear down buildings, the expense of which was to be met by a tax or rental of six pence on the pound for five years, and two pence for ten years longer. This tax was reduced to four pence after the first year. The ground purchased was cleared, streets were laid out and the property was resold to be built on by new owners. The financial management was admirable. Three hundred and fifty thousand pounds, raised by taxation, furnished sufficient capital for all improvements, and the net cost to the city, including suits lost, interest on cost of land lying idle, and all expenses of management, is estimated at about one hundred and eighty thousand pounds. Artificial elevation of prices by land owners, in view of a sale to the city, was avoided by judicious management. All bargains were made individually, by a private agent, and no striking improvement, which should enhance the value of the land at any given point, was undertaken until all the land affected by it had been purchased.

Tenants in the purchased dwellings were not evicted until places could be found for them elsewhere. The knowledge that they were to be dispossessed caused the erection of buildings and tenements for them where land was available, in the outskirts of the town. The result of these changes was that the centre of the city, in its reclaimed condition, was built up with shops and warehouses, or houses for the middle class, while the poorer classes were housed on the outskirts, a much healthier condition of things than had before existed.

Seven model tenements were erected at a cost of £90,000, but these were soon sold to private owners, as they were found to be unprofitable, because, being erected at the expense of the city, they were considered as public charities and were consequently unpopular.

The death rate, which had been 32.4 per thousand from 1868–70, fell to 25.5 per thousand from 1880–82. The number of crimes decreased from 10,899 in 1867 to 7,869 in 1873.

Five other towns, where expropriation has been tried, give the following results:

	Total cost of property.	Estimated loss.
Swansea	£61,280	£11,044
Wolverhampton	162,307	45,307
Derby	86,540	37,774
Nottingham	84,500	35,500
Newcastle-on-Tyne	40,000	18,300

From which we see that the average net charge was more than thirty per cent. on the original cost of the property.

In Birmingham forty-three acres in the worst districts were cleared, and a new street sixty-five feet wide was run from the heart of the city. The land was then leased on long leases. The former population was 9,000, comprised in 1,335 houses. In the first two years 4,904 small houses, accommodating 25,000 persons, were built by private enterprise. The death-rate decreased perceptibly, as may be seen from the following:

	Average 1873–75.	Average 79–81.
Bailey Street	97	25 6
Lower Priory	62	21 9
Aston Road	40	15
Russell Street	55	19

The total for eight streets showed a reduction from twenty-six per thousand to twenty per thousand, a saving of 2,400 lives per annum. Here the property

4

cost £1,474,000 and the net deficiency was $550,000, which was met by a tax of four pence on the pound. It seems to Mr. Chamberlain, who has spent much time in investigating this question, that some such laws as here outlined, should be passed and enforced:

It should be a misdemeanor to own unsanitary property.

Land bought by reason of expropriation should have a heavy fine for this misdemeanor deducted from the price.

Local authorities should have the power to close such buildings or make repairs at the cost of the owner without being compelled to acquire them.

The price paid should be that of the open market, valued by an official arbitrator.

The cost should be paid by the holders of adjacent property.

The effect of these provisions would be simply that improvements on a large scale, in very large towns, could be undertaken by the local authority without fear of excessive cost or additional burden on the tax payers.

Expropriation is a success in so far as it has lowered the death-rate and the crime of the cities where it has been tried.

A point in its favor is the fact that, by a systematic arrangement of blocks and houses a much larger population can be put upon the same area than by the present unsystematic method of construction. As an example, take the district of Westminster, which is the most populous in London. As originally built it accommodated only two hundred and thirty-five persons to the acre. When rebuilt to better advantage one thousand to the acre were accommodated.

That expropriation would be an extreme measure for America is generally admitted. It might, however, be beneficial on a small scale in such districts as are a menace to the health of the community. That it is unwise in principle is maintained by many able writers. "It is not the duty of the state," says Sir Richard Cross, "to provide good dwellings for the poor; if it did so, it would inevitably tend to make that class depend not on themselves, but on what was done for them elsewhere. Nor is it wise to encourage large bodies to provide the working class with habitations at greatly lower rents than the market value paid elsewhere. . . . . Any wholesale scheme of demolition only increases the evils of overcrowding, any attempt to lower rents would only cause a tendency to crowd (to that city). Any attempt to better the houses without bettering the manners would be useless."

Mr. Chamberlain says upon this question: "The cost is an insuperable obstacle at present to a bold and comprehensive dealing with the subject. It is simply a question between the rights of property and the rights of the community, and as long as we are willing to treat as one of the perquisites of private ownership the power of exacting extortionate terms of compensation whenever the necessities of the public call for expropriation, we may write as many articles and make as many speeches as we please about artisans' dwellings, but we shall not advance a single step in the direction of their improvement."

Expropriation has been many times suggested as a solution of the problem for this country, and probably it will be again. More lengthy discussion of this subject than it seems to warrant at first glance may, therefore, be justifiable.

Those who care to pursue the study of expropriation further will find many authorities on the subject. Expropriation has been tried in many of the countries of the continent, but the nature of this article must excuse the limitation of the discussion to England, where the situation is most like our own. A list of the more important English laws on this subject is appended.[1]

The many laws concerning expropriation have, in general, proved such expensive failures, that one is led to admire that ancient law of the Locrians, which compelled every proposer of a law to do so with a rope around his neck. But there are, however, laws that have proved effective in bringing unsanitary buildings to a healthy condition, and for preventing the erection of others.

The regulations of the health boards of New York and Brooklyn have, as it has been said, served as

[1]Lord Shaftesbury's Laboring Classes' Lodging House Acts, (with amendments), 1851, 1866, 1867, 1885.

Torrens Acts, 1868 and 1879, 31 and 32 Vict. C., 130; 42 and 43 Vict. C., 63 and 64.

Parts I and II of the Artisans' Dwelling Acts, 1882, 45 and 46 Vict. C., 54 and 56.

Lord Cross' Artisans' and Laborers' Dwelling Improvement Acts, 1879, 38 and 39 Vict. C., 36 and 64; 42 and 43 Vict. C., 63.

Nuisances Removal Acts, 1855 and 1858, 10 and 19 Vict. C., 121.

Public Health Acts, 1860, 1866, 1875, 29 and 30 Vict. C., 90 and 20; 23 and 24 Vict. C., 77.

Public Works Loan Act, 1879.

Sanitary Acts, 1866 and 1874.

Metropolitan Building Acts, 1855, 1860 and 1861.

models throughout the world. A short survey of them will therefore be more valuable than a review of those of other cities, which have for the most part been derived from them. An outline of the more important ones is here submitted:

A tenement-house is taken to mean every building, or portion thereof, which is rented to be occupied as a residence of three families or more, living independently of each other and doing their cooking upon the premises, or by more than two families upon any floor, so living and cooking, but having a common right in the halls, stairways, yards, water-closets or privies, or some of them.

Thousands of tenement buildings already constructed are compelled to conform to the requirements of the board.

A tenement may not be built on a lot with another building unless the clear space between the two is at least ten feet for one-story buildings, fifteen feet for two stories, twenty feet for three stories, twenty-five feet for buildings over three stories high.

No plan for light and ventilation of a tenement-house, with more than twelve rooms on five or more floors, intended to be erected on an ordinary city lot, except a corner lot, will be approved by the board of health if more than sixty-five percentum of the lot be covered, unless the courts to light and ventilate the interior rooms shall have an area of at least 265 square feet. Where there are to be twelve rooms on a floor the area of such courts must not be less than 215 square feet.

In the tenement buildings cellars must be whitewashed twice a year and be kept water tight, and must not be let as lodging rooms without a special permit, which regulates the height of the ceiling, number and size of the windows, etc. Cellars and yards must be keep free of garbage. Halls must open directly on the external air, or have sufficient light otherwise provided, and stairs must be furnished with railings. Proper receptacles for ashes and rubbish must be supplied.

In the rooms six hundred cubic feet of air must be provided for each occupant.

Rooms must be at least eight feet high; attic rooms must be eight feet in half of their area.

The total area for windows must be at least one-tenth of the superficial area of the room. The top must be seven and a-half feet above the ground and the upper half must open.

All sleeping rooms must have a window opening on external air, or a transom of three square feet over the door communicating with a room with such window, and also a transom of the same area opening on the hall.

Every building must have a ventilator of approved pattern in the roof at the top of the hall, and must be furnished with a fire-escape.

Drainage and plumbing plans of all buildings must be submitted and approved.[1]

There must be water on every floor.

There must be at least one water-closet for every fifteen occupants. Water-closets, sinks, cisterns,

---

[1] For special regulations as to sufficient plumbing see the "Sanitary Code," Sections 3 (as amended August 18, 1887), 17 (as amended March 4, 1881), 18 (as amended January 27, 1888), 19 (as amended March 4, 1881), 20, 22, 91, 92, 95 (as amended March 29 and May 19, 1887), 190 and 193 (adopted October 9, 1877, and amended November 27, 1877), 203 (adopted March 4, 1879), 206 (amended August 24, 1887), 211–18 inclusive (adopted August 18, 1887.)

pumps, sewers, privy-vaults, vaults and cess-pools must conform to regulation.

All tenements must be carefully inspected twice a year. All infectious and contagious diseases must be immediately reported.

The board of health has the power to vacate buildings which do not conform to its regulations. It has the power also to compel the employment of a resident janitor.

The owner shall be *prima facie* liable for the fines imposed for violation of any of these provisions, after him the lessee of the tenement.[1]

The increased area required for light and ventilation for interior rooms, and the adoption of the amendments to the plumbing code, which requires the plumbing to be of the highest degree of perfection, are due to the enlightenment of public opinion, which has been taken advantage of and utilized by the board of health.

President Bayles, of the health department, in a report transmitted to the legislature, states that, in his opinion, the two great advances in sanitation, viz.: the requirement of increased area for light and

[1] "It sometimes happens that a house is in litigation, or that the owner cannot be found, or if found, is so averse to making improvements as to render it necessary for the sanitary superintendent to make a personal inspection and to certify to the board that the premises are in a condition detrimental to health and dangerous to life by reason of defective plumbing and drainage or want of repair. Upon the filing of such certificate the board may declare the house unfit for human habitation and order it vacated within ten days. Such order of vacation is served upon the owner and occupants, as well as pasted on the front door of the house. If within the ten days the necessary repairs are not made or in progress the order is enforced. It rarely happens that before the expiration of the ten days the repairs are not commenced."—Report of Board of Health for 1891.

ventilation in interior rooms, and of plumbing of the highest degree of perfection, are due to the enlightenment of public opinion, which has been utilized by the board of health. Changes in construction are not allowed, after plans are once approved, unless such changes are also approved. Violations of these requirements render the offender liable to arrest, and in many cases to considerable fines. Enforcement of these regulations requires constant and persistent watchfulness of every detail.

Changes by builders in construction, from plans approved by the board, are not allowed, except when such changes, with modifications, have been submitted to and approved by the board. Violations in this regard, and of plumbing specifications, are followed by severe measures and penalties, even to the removal of entire walls and of defective plumbing. Large numbers of these violations have been discovered from time to time, and the guilty plumbers and builders have been arrested, and in many cases fined to a considerable amount, by order of the board. No amount of danger to public health seems to be a sufficient preventive of bad plumbing; on the other hand, the cupidity of indifferent plumbers in making contracts, under the competition for lowest bids, constantly presents inducements to violate the terms of the specifications whenever it can possibly be done without observation. This, of course, requires the most constant and persistent watchfulness of every detail upon the part of the officers of the board, and it is a matter of regret that, until recently, the force has been totally inadequate to assure absolute compliance with the plans and specifications of houses in course of construction.

This supervision cannot be performed in a per-
functory manner; on the contrary, it requires the
closest, most careful inspection by experts in respect
of all the details in the plumbing and drainage system of each house. It is an acknowledged fact that
these requirements for plumbing and drainage by the
health department of this city are far in advance of
those of any other city, and have become a standard
for other cities throughout the country and in many
of the European capitals.

One of the provisions of the tenement act of 1887
requires an inspection of every tenement and
lodging-house at least twice a year. The manner in
which this is complied with by the sanitary police is
described at length in President Bayles' report.[1] He
is of the opinion also that the department has enough
authority, stating that any important addition to
their powers would be an embarrassment.

The great improvement caused by these regulations may be seen by comparing the mortality in the
tenements of New York in 1869, when it was 28.35,
and in 1888, when it had fallen to 22.71.

The death-rate of children under five years of age,
the sure index of unsanitary conditions, exhibits in a
very satisfactory way the great benefits of tenement-
house reform. In 1866 the proportion of deaths of
children under five years of age to the total population was one in 69.93 +; in 1876 one in 74.28 +, and
in 1886 one in 89.26 +. The total of all deaths to
the population was in 1866 one in 33 + and in 1886
one in 38.52 +. Thus it may be seen, that with

---

[1] "Tenement House Problem in New York," transmitted to the
legislature January 16, 1888, by J. C. Bayles, president of the
board of health.

children during the last twenty years there has been a gain of one in 19.43 +, and in the total population of one in 5 +, notwithstanding the scourging of the city by two great epidemics of cholera and small-pox.

Powerful as the laws are, they require a much stronger backing of enlightened public opinion to make them as effective as they might be. So long as the owners and landlords feel that they have a right to do as they please with their own, and regard any interference by the health authorities as an encroachment on their rights as property-owners, the powers of the board will be greatly limited. They must be made to realize that it is as wrong to tolerate an unsanitary building which is dangerous to human life, as it is to encourage and countenance acknowledged crimes.

Mr. Riis, in "How the Other Half Lives," suggests a possible means of improvement:

"To remedy the over-crowding, which the night inspections of the sanitary police cannot keep step with,[1] tenements may eventually have to be licensed, as now the lodging-houses, to hold so many tenants, and no more, or the state may have to bring down the rents that cause the over-crowding by assuming the right to regulate them, as it regulates the fares on the elevated roads. I throw out the suggestion, knowing well that it is open to attack."

The wisdom of the scheme, often proposed, of encouraging the building of model tenements, by subsidies or a rebate in taxes on such property, seems to me very questionable.

In summing up this method of improving the homes of the poor, I cannot do better than quote the words on this subject in "Improved Dwellings for the Laboring Classes."

---

[1] During the quarter ending March 31, 1891, 10,334 night inspections were made.— *City Record, No.* 5,480. During 1891 54,643 inspections were made.—Report of Board of Health, 1891.

"Legislation may accomplish much, but let us guard against so easy an excuse for inaction. It is useless to legislate present houses out of existence, if better ones are not forthcoming. Let some better houses be built first and less legislation will be necessary to improve existing unhealthy buildings; for, of one hundred thousand families in present tenement-houses, it is safe to say that three-quarters will move gladly into better accommodations, as soon as these are provided. If even a few such blocks were built, the landlords would hasten to copy their improvements ere their houses should lose their tenants. No law can be enforced so rigidly as the law of supply and demand. There is no official mandate so powerful as self-interest and no courts so omnipotent as competition."

V.

The Reformation of Existing Buildings.

At the basis of the problem of the better housing of the poor lies this fundamental question: Are the poor in such a condition as to be willing to avail themselves of better accommodations, and qualified to use them to good advantage if offered them; or do they desire nothing better than those to which they have been accustomed?

Undoubtedly there are thousands who are unwilling to be helped. Dragged by main force out of their misery, it is but a short time before they return to their old ways. Accustomed all their lives to dirty surroundings and to perfect freedom, these unfortunates do not feel at home in clean apartments, whose very cleanliness is a constant reproach. They, who have never been bound by any laws, rebel at the many restraints, which are regarded by them as infractions upon their personal liberty.

It is hard for us to place ourselves in the position of these poor creatures. Born and bred amid surroundings where laws of every kind are unknown or laughed at, it would be strange, indeed, if they had any desire for improvement, which could be gained only by submission to restraint. We can not wholly realize what it is to be entirely without the restraint of any law but that of force.

In some of the many instances in which four or five families herd together in one small room, parents and children of all ages and both sexes live together entirely unmindful of moral laws. Cleanliness of person or rooms is wholely forgotten. The floors become littered with filth, for no one feels the desire or obligation to have it otherwise. The rights of property are disregarded or are only respected through fear of personal force.

Such a state of society can exist only when all desire to improve is absent. Its very existence of necessity postulates contentment. Why then should a person brought up amid such surroundings desire a change ?

To them cleanliness is bought only by an expenditure of time and labor to attain something which they never desired, and consequently would never miss. Healthful surroundings are not valued because unhealthful ones seem equally attractive.

These are the people who are the despair of property owners, and force even the most well-disposed of them to consider the expenditure on repairs and health appliances as money thrown away.

In many instances where tenements have been fitted out by their philanthropic owners with sanitary plumbing, stationary tubs, wood closets and all the latest improvements, if a watchful agent is not on the premises, all these appliances for the comfort and

health of the tenants are abused to such an extent
that they have to be removed, while in some instances
the pipes and other plumbing are stolen and sold for
junk, and the wood closets are used for kindling
wood.

Experience has proven the existence of a class of
the poor who can not be helped by removing them to
better surroundings. How, then, are they to be aided?
The problem has been successfully solved by Miss
Octavia Hill, who, as early as 1864, began in London
her efforts towards this end. She has reached the
conclusion that this class of people is not fit for better
accommodations, and can only very gradually become
so. From the many articles which have appeared over
the signature of Miss Hill during the last twenty-five
years, the following description of her methods has
been compiled. Those who would make a further
study of the question will find the names of such
articles in the bibliography.

Miss Hill purchases, from time to time, buildings
out of repair, especially those which are filled with
the lowest class that has any settled habitation.

The houses are put in order, but no new appliances
of any kind are added. The tenants must wait for
these until they have proven themselves capable of
taking care of them. A fixed sum is set aside for
repairs; if any of it remains after breakage and damage have been made good, each tenant in turn decides
in what way the surplus shall be spent, so as to add
to the comfort of the house. This plan has worked
admirably; the loss from carelessness has decreased
to a great extent, and the lodgers prize the little comforts which they have waited for, and seem in a
measure to have earned by their care, much more

than those bought with more lavish expenditure.
Thus the tenants are brought gradually to a higher
grade, and by the time that rebuilding is necessary,
they are in a condition to preserve and use to the
best advantage the better facilities which they then
enjoy.

The pecuniary result has been very satisfactory;
five per cent. interest has been paid on the capital
invested and a fund for the repayment of capital is
accumulated. This is attributed to two causes: first,
the absence of middlemen, and secondly, to great
strictness about punctual payment of rent. The bad
debts have been exceedingly small, the great want of
rooms giving the possessors immense powers over the
lodgers. Miss Hill does not force her attentions upon
her tenants. She has always made it a principle to
maintain perfect strictness in business relations, perfect respectfulness in personal relations.

This system appears at first thought incapable of
solving the problem, but we must remember that it is
meant that it should be applied on a very extended
scale. Miss Hill says, in explanation of the system:

"You may say, perhaps, this is very well as far as you and your
small knot of tenants are concerned, but how does it help us to deal
with the masses of poor in our great towns?" I reply: "Are
not the great masses made up of many small districts? Are there
not people who would gladly come forward to undertake the
systematic supervision of some house or houses, if they could get
authority from the owner? And why should there not be some way
of registering such supervision, so that, bit by bit, as more volunteers should come forward, the whole metropolis might be mapped
out, all the pieces fitting in like bits of mosaic to form one connected
whole?

"The success of the plan does not depend entirely upon the houses
being the property of the superintendent. I would urge people, if
possible, to purchase the houses of which they undertake the
charge; but if they cannot, they may yet do a valuable work by reg.
istering the distinct declaration that they will supervise such and
such a house, or row, or street."

It is needless to say, so well known have become Miss Hill's efforts in this direction, that her success has far exceeded her anticipations.

Miss Hill's method of beginning with the improvement of the individual rather than of the surroundings has had many advocates in this country.

Although they will eventually be destroyed by the progress of trade, or driven out of business by the competition with better houses, old tenements will exist for a long time. It is important, therefore, to consider how these buildings may be improved and put into a sanitary condition. A good example is here given, an account of which I quote:

"Few places have ever borne a worse name than Gotham Court in New York city. This famous block of buildings, next to the largest tenement in New York, is located at 36 and 38 Cherry street. It abuts on the street, running in 234 feet, with an alley nine feet wide on one side and seven on the other. Up to 1880 its record for disease, disorder, drunkenness and crime was almost unparalleled. In 1880 the property was leased by Messrs. D. Willis James, William E. Dodge and W. Bayard Cutting, who made extensive repairs and improvements. At that time there remained only 53 tenants; there are now 123, all apartments being let. The tenants are mostly Irish. Notwithstanding the general character of the neighborhood and the old reputation of the house, the halls, stairs and apartments are all kept wonderfully clean, and together with the demeanor of the tenants toward the ladies in charge of the building, testify to the uplifting power which a quiet, firm and sagacious woman can exercise upon the characters and habits of the poorest classes in the worst districts by assuming the duties of landlord or agent. Rents now range from $3 to $8 monthly, and the rent return in 1881 and 1882 was 6½ per cent. on the investment.

In striking contrast to this success, a word may be said of the neighboring 'Big Flats' at 98 Mott street. This building, the only tenement in the city larger than Gotham Court, was erected in 1884 as a model dwelling, and was in its construction a great advance over then existing tenements. Dust and dirt cover the stairs like a carpet, so that the hard stone steps are soft to the tread. Of the ninety-two apartments twenty-two are vacant; the rest are occupied by a mixed population of Polish Jews, Irish, Italians and Chinese.

The rental of three rooms and a pantry on the second floor is $9.75 per month. It appears, however, that at no time have the 'Big Flats' had an agent equal to the preservation of peace or the enforcement of any rules. The moral is plain: A well-built house with fire-proof halls and iron stairways, will become the residence of the lowest and dirtiest classes, unless the manager or agent leads or compels them to habits of neatness and order. A building must be not only made good, but kept good; rules must not only be framed but enforced.''

Another well-known instance of the improvement of low tenements through personal influence is the experience of Miss Ellen Collins, who bought a block of six houses on the corner of Water and Roosevelt streets, one of the worst localities in New York city. Some of these buildings were formerly dance halls, and were the resort of the worst characters. Now they are the most orderly in the neighborhood, and their influence on the surroundings is most beneficial. To quote from a letter by Miss Collins:

''The cost of the three tenement-houses, my first purchase in Water street, when refitted, was $21,179. I have had them under my care for five years. The total amount of rent received during five years, to May 1, 1885, is $12,895.08, the total loss $190.93.

''For the three years ending May 1, 1885, the net return was over 6 per cent. per annum on the investment.

''There are 31 families now in the houses. Of these

15 have been there for 5 years.
1   "   "   " 4 "
5   "   "   " 3 "

''There never has been any need of putting up a bill; as soon as a suite of rooms is vacant some one applies for it. The success with the store has been less constant.

''Careful superintendence, locking of street doors after 10 o'clock at night, and a gas-light burning in the yard all night have quite redeemed the place from ill repute as a haunt of thieves. Clothes are left hanging on the lines all night with impunity, and women have said that they can sleep as quietly as I can in my own home.

''Open windows in the entries beside the sinks have broken up the habit of accumulating refuse on the floors. Having all the water-closets in the yard keeps the air of the houses free from bad smells.

"The three houses first named have twenty-four suites, consisting of one living and two sleeping rooms, and eight suites with only one bed-room each. In three instances one family has two suites, making a whole floor; the prices vary from $3.50 to $8.

"In view of the tendency to add 'modern conveniences,' and thus increase the expense, my judgment favors the refitting of old houses rather than building new ones. As the main feature of the work is personal supervision of details, there is much greater probability of success when it is undertaken by individuals rather than by corporations, where responsibility, except in the matter of expense, is too often and too easily lost sight of."

In Boston Mrs. Lincoln has met with similar success, which she thus describes in a letter:

"Five years ago it was my privilege to hire (with a friend) a well known but ill-managed tenement-house in one of the most crowded parts of Boston. Our object in taking the house was to see whether, by close supervision and a strict adherence to rules, we could improve the condition of the tenants, and also secure a fair return upon the amount invested.

"In this house there are twenty-seven tenements, containing on an average eighty-three people. When we first took it it had been notorious for many years, and had to live down its evil reputation, and it took some little time to convince tenants who applied for rooms that its character for lawlessness was about to be redeemed, and that no one would be admitted or allowed to remain in the building who would not abide by the rules.

"The standard of the house became higher. We asked and readily obtained higher rents for the rooms, and, in consequence, were able to offer the tenants greater advantages.

"The demand for rooms increased and vacancies were infrequent. A spirit of order began to replace the reign of lawlessness, and an interest in the common welfare of the house and its inmates began to show itself among the tenants.

"My experience has been that even very cheap and poor tenement-houses can be made to pay. Mine are both wooden buildings, unattractive enough in externals, but possessing within them the materials for comfortable homes for very poor people.

"My opinion, formed slowly, has come to be that old and dilapidated houses should be improved and cared for by one or two people. Little capital is required; only time and attention from one or two, who are enough interested to give a constant supervision to the condition of the houses and their occupants. A com-

5

pany is needed to raise money, to buy and build houses, but old houses can be hired by individuals.

"A tenement-house need not be a source of annoyance to the neighborhood. A few years ago there were constant complaints of the noise and drunkenness of the inmates of the first house, which I and my friend afterward hired. I think I can safely assume that neither of my houses is now considered an objectionable element in the neighborhood. The tenants, although very poor, are respectable, and have learned to respect the rights of others, thus winning regard for their own.

"This result has been brought about slowly and by degrees. We did not attempt too much at once. We expected to improve the character of the inmates as we did that of the house, gradually. It has been my experience that tenants of this class often need only the stimulus which interest and sympathy give, to enable them to do better.

"A strict adherence to principles and rules, which are laid down for the benefit of all, a quick sense of justice, friendly interest in the welfare of the tenants, a recognition of the fact that there are obligations on both sides—these seem to me of the elements of success in the management of a tenement-house."

In Philadelphia Miss Edith Wright obtained control of forty-one houses with 250 occupants. These houses had acquired a reputation for dirt and disorder, while the surroundings were as unhealthy as possible. A great change has been wrought, and the houses have become as noticeable for their cleanliness as they were formerly for their filth.

The efforts of the settlement societies to elevate the condition of the poor have an important bearing on this subject. These go under the names of Social, University and College settlements, and have as their aim the education of the poor. The children are taught in the schools and kindergartens, and the elder ones are given amusement and instruction by the use of gymnasiums, concerts, lectures and the like. In this way they are insensibly led out of their old tastes and habits, and the desire for better things is inculcated.   With education comes a desire for better dwellings and for a better home life than that which they have been accustomed to.

Toynbee Hall, in East London, the first of these attempts, was followed by the establishment of similar institutions in various parts of England.   In America have been founded such well-known "settlements" as Hull House in Chicago, presided over by Miss Jane Addams, who has described her efforts in the *Forum* of October and November, 1892, and the Rivington Street Settlement in New York, the managers of which, in a pamphlet lately published (December, 1892), outline its history and the success it has achieved.

Investigation shows us the existence in our cities of persons so ignorant, unambitious or vicious that they are unfitted to occupy any dwellings other than the most squalid.   Experience proves that these persons may be so improved by personal influence that they will not only use to advantage whatever improvements may be furnished them, but will constantly demand something better.

This result will obtain only by long continued and well directed efforts of those who are willing to give the work their constant attention.

VI.

The Single Tenement.

The tenement erected upon a single lot will probably always play an important part in the housing of our poor.   It is often the ambition of those who were formerly the occupants of tenements, but who have in some way become possessed of a little money, to own a tenant-house and become proprietors themselves; for they know best how profitable the business is. Possessed of but little means, it is not strange that the single lot tenement alone is within their reach, and that the buildings erected by them are of cheap construction.

To illustrate the gradual but constant improvement of construction with reference to light and air, the plans of a number of tenements are given, which have been approved by the New York health department from 1879 to the present time.

Prior to that date, it must be remembered, light shafts were not compulsory, and as many rooms were crowded upon the lot as possible, without thought of supplying their inmates with light and air other than could be obtained by the door connecting the various rooms in the suite with the front room, which was usually occupied as a kitchen.

Figure 2 shows one of the first plans in which light shafts were introduced, but even here the four interior rooms depend on transoms opening into adjacent rooms for their ventilation.

Figure 3 shows a better arrangement; here all rooms give either on the open air or upon light shafts.

Figure 4 illustrates one of the many attempts to economize by grouping four rooms about an interior shaft.

In the plan illustrated by Figure 5 the stud partitions have been replaced by brick ones, and the staircase and water-closets are well lighted.

In 1879 the *Plumber and Sanitary Engineer* offered prizes aggregating $500 for the best designs for tenement-houses upon a lot 25′x100′. Figure 6 shows

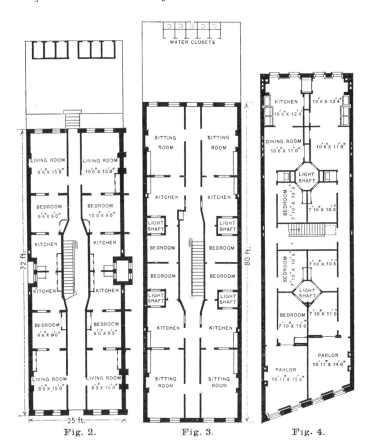

Fig. 2.   Fig. 3.   Fig. 4.

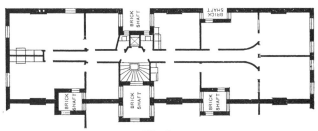

Fig. 5.

the first-story plan, and Figure 7 the second-story of the design, which won in the competition.

It is most encouraging to note the advance in construction of the tenement since that day. It is doubtful whether a building on these plans would be erected at the present time, for the interior rooms are wholly dependent upon adjoining rooms for their ventilation.

The committee which awarded the prizes emphatically declared that, in their view, it was impossible to secure light and air, the requisites of physical and moral health, within these narrow and arbitrary limits.

Figures 8, 9 and 10 show various plans for the accommodation of four families on a single floor, on what is termed the dumb-bell plan.

Figure 11 adopts the method of placing the courts on either side, and continuing them to the open air in the rear, thus insuring better ventilation.

In the plan illustrated by Figure 12 provision is made for six families on a single floor, but interior air-shafts are employed.

Figure 13 illustrates a tenement covering a larger area. Here all rooms are well lighted and aired, and the windows are arranged to insure the greatest privacy possible.

As may be seen by the health reports, by far the greatest number of tenements built every year are upon a single lot. It is therefore important to consider the construction of the single tenement which is of maximum convenience and healthfulness.

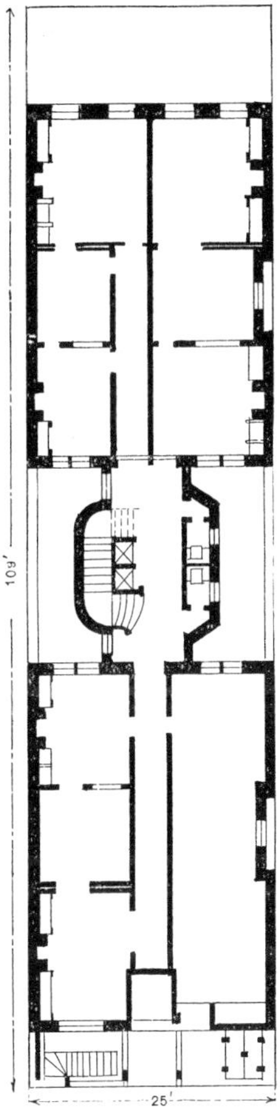

Fig. 6.

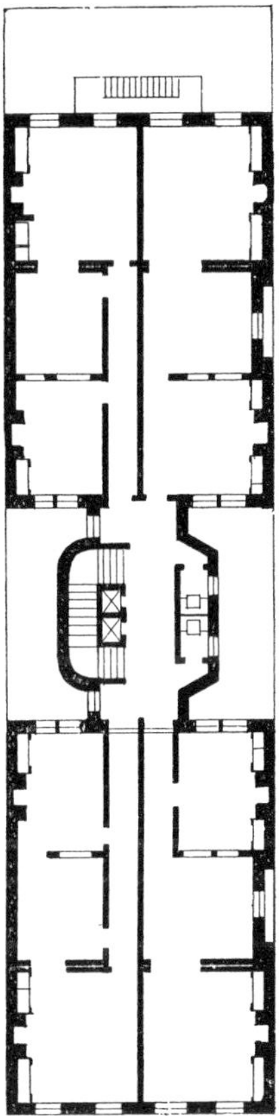

Fig. 7.

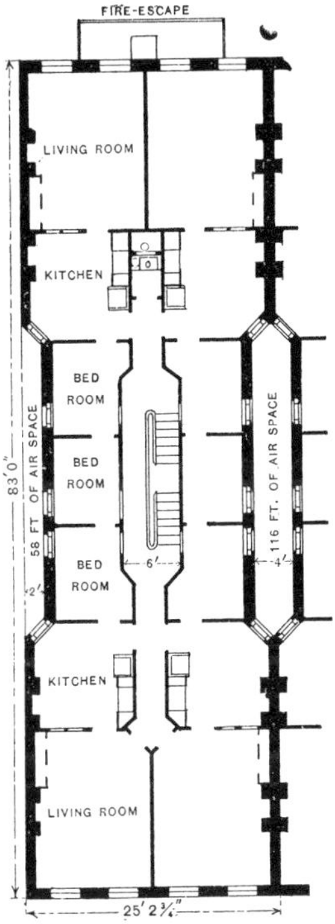

Fig. 8.

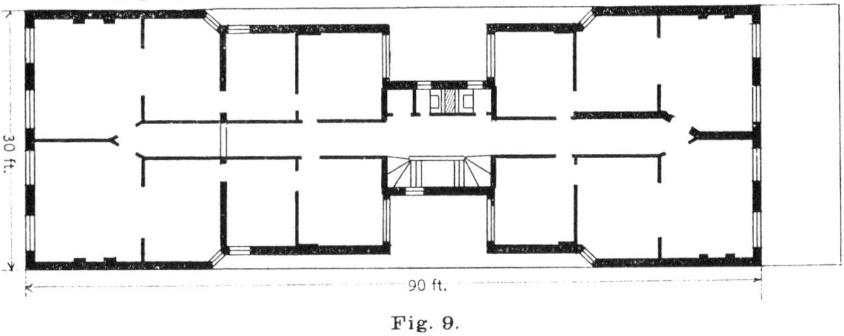

Fig. 9.

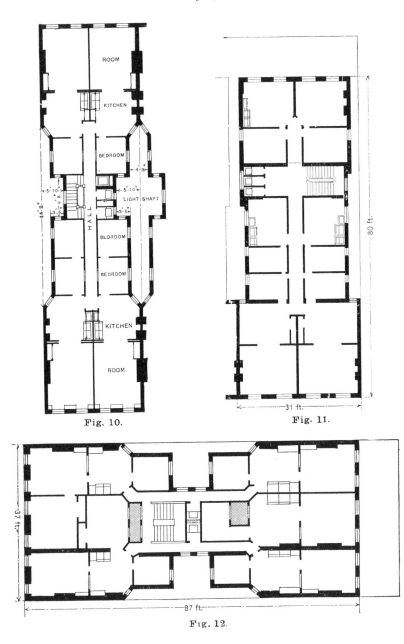

Fig. 10.

Fig. 11.

Fig. 12.

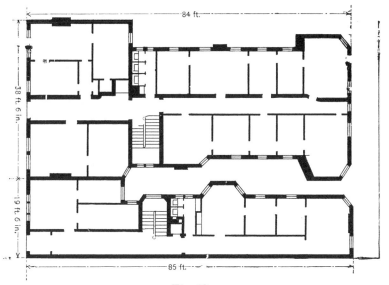

Fig. 13.

The five important principles in the construction of such a tenement are:

1. Each sleeping room should have direct exterior light and air.

2. Interior light and air shafts should be avoided if possible.

3. Communication between the several rooms should be independent.

4. The common halls should be as wide as space will permit.

5. The stairway should be direct, easy of ascent, without "winders" and well lighted and ventilated.[1]

On the ordinary lot (25 x 100) it is exceedingly difficult to meet these requirements in a satisfactory manner.

[1] "The City Residence." Chap. II. W. B. Tuthill, from which volume these illustrations are reproduced.

Single tenements may be roughly divided, as to plan, into four groups, determined by the respective situation of the shaft or well, as follows:

a Those that are bilateral. (See Fig. 14.)

b Those that have a central shaft enclosed on four sides. (See Fig. 15.)

c Those with a central well enclosed on three sides, but open in the rear. (See Fig. 16.)

d Those with a deep shaft at the centre of one side. (See Fig. 17.)

Fig. 14.　　　Fig. 15.　　　Fig. 16.　　　Fig. 17.

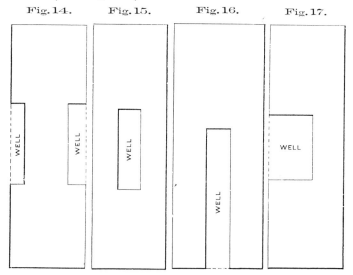

These shafts should, for ventilation, have some connection at the bottom with the outside air. When nothing better can be had, air may be furnished by ducts similar to the cold air boxes used in furnaces.

All interior shafts should have an area proportional to their depth. The effective shaft would, therefore, have the vertical section, as indicated in Figure 18.

Fig. 18.

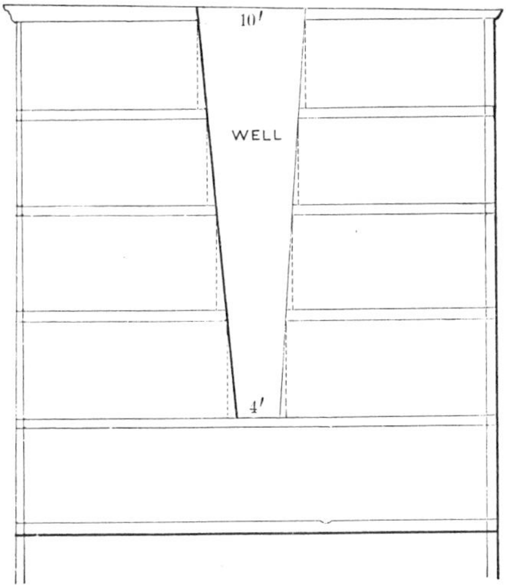

Four plans, as given in Tuthill, typical of the various positions of the air shafts, are here appended, and their relative advantages will now be considered:

(1.) Bilateral well-holes. (See Fig. 19.) This arrangement is very popular, because it meets the letter of the law at the least expense of plan room. The front and rear rooms are the reverse of one another. The living rooms and large sleeping rooms open on the street or yard, the kitchens and smaller bedrooms on the well. Stairway, water-closets and lift are in the neck of the building, and receive ample ventilation from the court. The first story is devoted in front to two stores, the central hall leading to the rear apartments. This plan meets the requirements fairly well, if the air shafts are of a decent width.

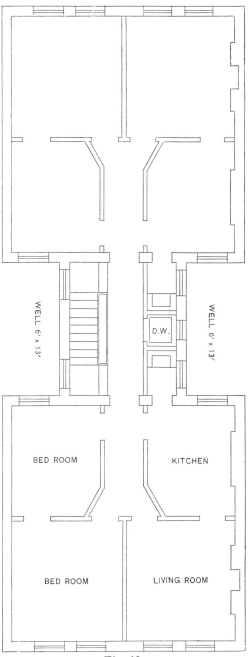

Fig. 19.

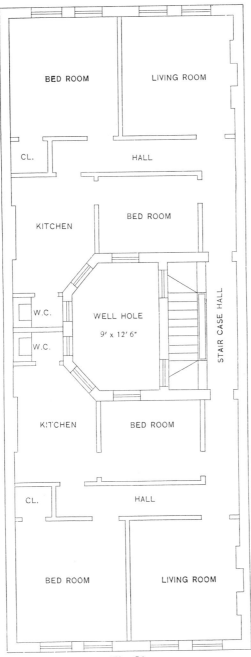

Fig. 20.

(2.) Central well-hole. (See Fig. 20.) The living and main bedrooms open as before on direct light, the smaller bedrooms and kitchens on the well. The water-closets, being adjacent, require but a single line of pipe. The main objection is that much space is given to the halls, which, however, is not without its advantages in securing increased privacy.

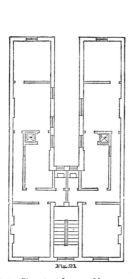

(3.) Central well enclosed on only three sides. (See Fig. 21.) This arrangement of the well has better advantages in respect to light and air, as ventilation, without the use of air ducts, is here possible. The stairs are also in a position to receive direct external light, but the width of the bilateral rooms is consequently diminished. The dark passage, back of the kitchen, and leading to the living room, is objectionable, as is also the absence of direct communication with the second bedroom.

(4.) Court at the side of the building. (See Fig. 22.) By this arrangement better light and ventilation is afforded than by any of the others. The great advantage of this plan is that, when a succession of such houses is built, by a reversal of the plans the two wells may be made adjacent, a fairly large court results, in which a circulation of air is insured. This is true of the first type, but to a less degree.

The actual ground space covered by each and the size of the light wells are here given:

Plan No. 1—Ground covered, 1444 square feet; well, 156 square feet. Number of feet of wall, 228.

Plan No. 2—Ground covered, 1481 square feet; well, 119 square feet. Number of feet of wall, 236.

Plan No. 3—Ground covered, 1469 square feet; well, 211 square feet. Number of feet of wall, 271.

Plan No. 4—Ground covered, 1406 square feet; well, 194 square feet. Number of feet of wall, 232.

In Chicago there are comparatively few large tenements, and no marked disposition is shown to build them. There are thousands of two story frame houses, each one more or less crowded with occupants, but surrounded by ample air space, and standing in a lot by itself, or with only a rear cottage besides.

These small houses are the remains of earlier days, and have, many of them, been removed on rollers from street to street.

The few new tenements in course of construction are for the most part three-story brick buildings, with light in front, rear and on one side. The municipal ordinances concerning light and air are very inadequate, so that it would be very unfortunate if large tenements were built with no more regard to sanitation than the health laws would require. As it happens, however, few unsanitary buildings are built, and for this reason the need of model tenements has not been felt so urgently as in other cities.

The worst feature of the present brick structures is the basement dwelling, which, though scarcely below the street level, is naturally more damp and dark than a ground or upper floor.

In June, 1892, rents varied from $2.75 a month for one room in a rear basement, to $14 for four rooms, one dark, and $18 for seven rooms and bath. The cheapest rooms are occupied by Italians and Russian Hebrews, the English-speaking occupants of such quarters being exceedingly few.

The small tenement has been described and illustrated at length, not because the writer approves of this method of housing our poorer classes, but because, under existing conditions, the single tenement will largely predominate over all others.

I am, however, positive that complete success cannot attend any effort to provide our poor with clean, healthy homes upon the lines of the single tenement.

Sun and air are necessary conditions, and to expect to provide these upon any plan which is limited to lots 25'x100', is to expect the impossible.

VII.

THE MODEL TENEMENT.

However necessary good laws, well enforced, and however valuable personal influence may be, it is the large tenement, constructed on sanitary methods, that will be the most effective in doing the most good to the greatest number.

England tried the experiment and set us the example thirty years ago; but it was not followed in this country for fully fifteen years, and even now we are far behind in the number of model tenements. As we have much to learn from England it will be profitable briefly to examine the progress of the most important model tenement companies there, especially as more attention has there been paid to collecting accurate information as to death-rates, sickness, etc.

The late Mr. Peabody gave in 1862, £150,000 as a fund for the erection of sanitary homes for the London poor. In 1866 and 1868 he gave £100,000, and by bequest in 1873 £150,000, making a total of £500,000. The trustees wisely regarded this as a perpetual advance of capital rather than as a gift, and their buildings have always brought them in the three per cent. to which their dividends have been limited, so that at the beginning of the present year the fund had increased to £1,023,446.

The trustees purchased the land required at exceptionally advantageous rates, paying the board of works five shillings a foot, although it cost the latter a guinea a foot. As has been shown in the outline of expropriations in England, its market value was by no means as high as the sum paid by the board. The cost of each room of the Peabody buildings has been found to be £75, of which about £25 was for the land.

The popularity of these buildings is shown by the fact that when the Bedfordbury buildings were opened, 2,500 applied for the 146 dwellings. At the close of last year the trustees were providing homes for 20,462 persons, who were contained in 11,275

6

rooms. These comprised 5,071 separate dwellings,[1] viz.: 75 of 4 rooms, 1,789 of 3 rooms, 2401 of 2 rooms and 806 of 1 room. The average weekly earnings of the head of each family in residence at the close of the year was £1, 3s. 8¼d. The average rent of each dwelling was 4s. 9¼d. per week, and of each room 2s. 1¾d. The rent in all cases includes free use of water, laundries, sculleries and bath rooms.

"The birth-rate for the year 1891 reached 38.49 per 1,000, which is 9.41 per thousand above the average of London for the same period. The death-rate, including the deaths of 70 inhabitants of the buildings who were removed to hospitals was 21.15 per 1,000, which is 0.85 per 100 below the average of London. This is fortunately an exceptional circumstance, and is due to the epidemic of last spring, from which many of the tenants suffered. The infant mortality was 141.22 per 1,000 births, or 21.39 below that of London."

The death-rate in the Peabody buildings as compared with that of all of London was as follows: 1880, 17 against 21.9; 1881, 17.22 against 21.20; 1882, 18.42 against 21.40. These are not selected as especially favorable years, but merely because they came to my notice. The second most important association of this character is the Improved Industrial Dwellings Company, which was incorporated in 1863, and of whose board of directors Sir Sydney Waterlow has been the chairman for many years. The capital consists of £500,000, but loans from the Public Works Loan Commissioners and elsewhere bring the total to £1,061,991. The average cost of the rooms erected by this company has been about £51. In size they average 130 square feet, being usually 9 x 12 or 13 x 12, and containing about 1,000 cubic feet of air. (The London laws require 400 cubic feet in living rooms

---

[1] "Twenty-sixth Annual Report of the Peabody Donation Fund" (1891).

and 300 cubic feet in sleeping rooms.) The essential principle in their arrangement is that each tenement shall be absolutely complete in itself. The death-rate in the company's buildings for sixteen years averages 16.7 as against 23.4 in the city. The density of population is about 750 per acre; in the city it is 42 per acre.

"The mortality returns of the company's buildings continue to show the most favorable and encouraging results. For the year ending June 30, 1890, the average death-rate, according to statistics received from the registrar of births and deaths, was only 11.6 in the 1.000, including 4.4 of infants under one year of age, while, excepting a few cases of infantile diseases, as whooping cough, measles, etc., there were only ten deaths from contagious or infectious diseases at the 41 estates in occupation. The birth-rate in the buildings averaged 31.1 per 1,000. The average death-rate in the metropolis was 18.8 per 1,000—although in low and overcrowded districts it was probably between 30 to 40 per 1,000—and the birth-rate was 29.7 per 1,000. At the company's large estate at Bethnal Green, while the birth-rate was 37.9, the death-rate reached only 8.5 per 1,000; and the latter, compared with the death-rate of 40 per 1,000, in the large area in the same neighborhood condemned by the county council, speaks volumes for the beneficent work which the company was established to carry out.

"The number of estates belonging to the company is 44, and when all the buildings are completed there will be separate accommodations for 5,339 families, or nearly 30,000 persons of the working classes, with 117 shops and 37 workshops, the whole representing a total equal to 18,645 rooms. The total outlay on capital account is estimated to reach £1,086,000."

The company also manages 323 improved dwellings belonging to private persons, and a number owned by similar associations, so that the total number of dwellings and shops under the control of the company is 5,790, which accommodates about 30,000 persons. The buildings have been divided into 12 suites of 6 rooms, 298 of 5 rooms, 2,955 of 3 rooms, 374 of 2 rooms and 28 single apartments.[1]

---

[1] Report of the Improved Industrial Dwellings Company, 1891.

Sir Sydney Waterlow does not believe in the policy of driving the laboring classes into the suburbs, and what he says of London on this point is equally true of New York and many other American cities.

"Among the artisan classes, the father of the family is, in the majority of cases, not the only bread-winner. In early married life the wife often continues for years to earn a few shillings per week, and in later years, when children have grown up, the boys go to work as errand boys, etc., and in this way the earnings of the father are largely supplemented. The father may ride to and from work by rail, but the earnings of the other members of the family will not bear this expense, and if they do not live near their work they get none at all. * * * When a mechanic lives near enough to work to take his meals at home his weekly wages find their way to the family purse to a much greater extent than they can do when a deduction has to be made from them, not only for meals taken in a public house but for other outgoings induced by the temptations of such a practice."

The Trustees of the Guinness Trust, 5 Victoria street, S. W., and the Artisans and Laborers' General Dwellings Company, 16 Great George street, S. W., are at present erecting large blocks of model tenements. Both the Metropolitan Association and the Improved Dwellings Company publish plans and descriptions of their buildings.

The merits of single-room tenements find a warm advocate in Miss Octavia Hill. According to that excellent authority, "the two or three-room tenements look hopelessly dear and unattainable to the laborer; he never goes near them, but shrinks into some back court or alley. Offer him one large room, * * * * and when his first boy or girl begins to add to the revenue let him take a little room opening on the same lobby. Every court I ever bought has been a one-roomed court. By experience in old houses one learns how to build new ones to fit the poorer people. Depend upon it,

if houses were built like this, a great many poor
would come to them.'' A diametrically opposite
stand is maintained and with good reason, it seems
to me, by Arnold White in his '' Problems of a Great
City,'' who thus concludes his remarks on this subject: '' The single-room system fosters incest, ille-
gitimacy, juvenile prostitution, drunkenness, dirt,
idleness and disease.'' A formidable array certainly.
Here are Sir Sydney Waterlow's opinions, if I may
be pardoned a further quotation on this subject, for
it is a most important one and most intimately connected with the first principles of the housing of our
poor:

" It is quite true I do not provide single rooms. But one of the
objects of these improved dwellings is to help to eradicate the
whole system of living of which these single-room dwellings are
the evil sign. We build for the future, and look forward to the
time when no family need be compelled to live in a single room.
It is impossible that either sanitary or moral conditions can ever
be satisfied under such a system. No proper feelings of decency or
self-respect can be cultivated in families living in a single room.
Yet even the unfortunate class which over-crowding forces into
single-room dwellings are helped and relieved by the provision of
more eligible tenements. The better class of working people are
glad to get out of such miserable dwellings into better ones, and, as
they do so, more room is left for the rest. It is the competition of
better-class workmen with the very poor which makes the rent of
bad dwellings so very high; diminish that competition and rents
will fall, and the owners of such property will be compelled by
the loss of tenants to effect improvements, which will never be
accomplished in any other way. Improvements of this kind must
begin from the top; if you simply draw out the worst layer from
below, those will sink into its place, while by taking away the
upper strata, those below, relieved from pressure, rise into their
vacant places. Even the poor widow, who can only pay two shillings a week for a single room, is thus most directly benefited.''

The movement to secure better and cheaper homes
for our poor by building large, well-appointed tenements took substance in America first in Brooklyn.

Here Mr. Alfred T. White was of the opinion that
the poor were ready for better homes, and that they
did not have to be educated up to them. As he himself emphatically put it: "They are up to them
now, fully, if the chances were only offered. They
do not have to come up. It is all a gigantic mistake
on the part of the public of which these poor people
are the victims." He had the means and the energy
to solidify his opinions into brick and mortar, and the
result was that his first block, the Home Buildings, on the corner of Hicks and Baltic streets, were
opened for occupation February 1, 1877.

The buildings met the popular demand and were at
once filled. The Brooklyn board of health published a most careful description of these buildings,
with plans and elevations, in their report of 1878.
Two years later the Tower buildings were erected.
As these then represented the highest development
of the tenement and embody most of the features
which have been found useful in England, as well
as those in the buildings erected later by the Improved Dwelling Company, this description is here
given, together with the comment on these tenements
in Mr. Alfred T. White's monograph:[1]

" In all of these buildings access to the upper stories is had by
staircases open to the front. The stairs are of slate and set in solid
brick work. In rising from story to story a half turn is made, and
at the top of each flight a slate balcony, protected by an iron rail-
ing, is reached. These balconies, in the first and third blocks, are
about thirty feet long. From each end of the balcony a hallway
or lobby runs back; private halls admitting to the rooms of each
dwelling lead from this hallway. Thus every family has its
dwelling, entirely private and apart from, and with no room opening into another, while all the rooms have direct sunlight. The
rooms are provided with closets, with hooks and shelves, and the

---

[1] "Improved Dwellings for the Laboring Classes."

living-room with a dresser and coal box to hold a quarter of a ton. Both sitting and living-rooms have fire-places and mantels. The height of ceilings is eight feet three inches in the clear. The windows of all the rooms are of unusual size and extend up close to the ceiling. From the living-room a door leads into the extension, a small room 7½ by 5 feet. This contains an ash flue, a sink, a stationary washtub, a window, and a water closet with separate outside window. All of these conveniences are furnished to every family apart from all others. The ash flues, one foot square and ventilated at the top, discharge into large ash-rooms in rear of the cellars, separated from main cellars by a brick wall, and accessible only by doors in the rear. No ashes or refuse is ever exposed on the sidewalk or elsewhere. All refuse is burned, and the ashes are loaded directly from the ash-vaults into carts, which pass out by a rear gateway. The water supply is ample and is carried up in a corner of the living-room, where the pipes are out of the reach of the frost. The water can be shut off from the sculleries by faucets placed in each apartment. The water closets are all provided with cisterns overhead to insure instant supply of water. The traps are ventilated, the siphoning prevented by vent-pipes carried above the roof. The washtubs and sinks are trapped separately from the water closets. The soil pipes are open at the roof, and serve as rain conductors. These pipes pass down against the back wall of the extension and out through the rear wall of the cellars into the sewer, avoiding any horizontal drains under the buildings. Every family has a large coal-bin and wood-bin in the cellar, numbered to correspond with its rooms. Hoisting tackle is provided for the use of the tenants. The buildings are all of good red brick, and all windows and outside doors are arched with brick. Floors are of the best yellow pine throughout. The flat gravel roof is used as a clothes-drying ground by the families in the three upper stories. For the occupants of the lower stories lines are provided in the yard. The slate staircase extending from cellar to roof, is not only absolutely fire-proof, but cannot be reached by any fire that may occur in the buildings, forming an unequalled fire escape.

"The front of the new block is much more ornamental and attractive than either of the others. Open towers rise from the ground to the roof, to afford better protection to the staircases, and add greatly to the appearance."

The various buildings of the company are: Homes Building, Hicks and Baltic streets, 80 dwellings, completed 1877; Tower Buildings, Warren and

Bactic streets, 76 dwellings, completed 1879; Warren Place, 8 nine-room houses, 26 six-room houses.

"Of the tenement dwellings there are 1 of six rooms, 25 of five rooms, 147 of four rooms, 45 of three rooms, total 218 dwellings. To which add 15 stores and 34 houses, and we find accommodations for 267 families in all, or say 1,000 people. The four-room dwellings comprise a living room, a scullery and two bed-rooms; the three-room dwellings a living-room (with alcove for bed), a scullery and a bed-room. The floors are arranged in exactly the same way in every respect, from the first story up to the top. This secures the greatest strength and stability, and also allows the duplication of all the parts by machinery, materially lessening the cost of construction.

"The average rentals in all the buildings are—

	Per Week.	Equivalent (less discount allowed). Per Month.
Four-room dwellings......	$1 93	$7 95
Three-room "	1 48	6 00
At the lowest rentals are—		
Four-room dwellings.	1 50	6 09
Three-room "	1 30	5 21

"The lowest rentals are of course on the top floor, and all rentals are increased ten cents per week for each floor moving downwards."

Tenants desiring at any time to pay the rent for four or more weeks in advance are allowed a deduction of ten cents per week in the rent so paid.

"The difficulty of accumulating for some weeks to pay the landlord is avoided by weekly instead of monthly payments, and landlord and tenants both gain by the arrangement. The liberal terms offered to those who pay for four weeks in advance are appreciated by the tenants, and many who could not avail themselves of the discount will lay by enough to secure it regularly hereafter. About one-fourth of the tenants have always taken the benefit of the discount, and another fourth have done so more than half the time; while over one-fourth, again, have never paid except from week to week. Every tenant having entire control of his own water facilities, there is no difficulty in fixing responsibility for any damage thereto, which is therefore sure to be a minimum. Where repairs are few, and where loss by non-payment will rarely, if ever, occur, good tenants need not pay for the deficiencies of bad ones, and rents can be kept low at a profit.

"Few day-laborers, even, pay a less rent than $6 or $7 per month, in the same neighborhood, for the ordinary accommodations. Here they have more floor space, with other advantages which make comparison impossible. Moreover, the complete family privacy of the apartments in this kind of building allows a mixture of different classes and nationalities which no common house can keep under the same roof; the mechanic, paying a good rent down stairs, helps to reduce the rent of the laborer, who is willing to go up a few flights, and who there finds the same accommodation within his means.

"A census of the 137 families residing in the Tower and Home buildings in 1879, revealed many very interesting points. The facility with which all classes can be suited in this style of improved dwellings is attested by the presence of fifteen nationalities. Of these Ireland was represented by 51 families, the United States by 40, England by 10, Sweden by 9 and Germany by 5.

"The occupations of the heads of families were thus classified: Storekeepers, 11; employed in stores, etc., 36; mechanics, 33; seafaring men, 18; women, 17; miscellaneous laborers, 15; miscellaneous, 7; total, 137.

"Of the 539 individuals composing these families, 75 were children between one and five years of age, and 37 were children less than a year old. The total number of children in New York city under the age of five years is estimated at less than one-eighth of the whole population; in the improved dwellings the proportion is, therefore, nearly twice the average. Remembering, then, that the ordinary average death-rate of children under five years is six times that of persons over five, we can recognize that a reduced total death-rate in these improved dwellings means a saving of child-life of vast importance."

The Riverside buildings have been erected on a similar plan (in 1890) since these descriptions were published, and are important as representing the highest development of the tenement-house.

Figures 23 and 24 show the plan and exterior of these buildings, and Figure 25 the plan of one portion on a larger scale.

The following description is from a late (1890) publication of the company erecting it:

"The Riverside buildings are situated on the slope from Brooklyn Heights to the East river, about midway between the Wall street and South ferries, and two minues walk from either.

"The frontage is 307 feet on Columbia Place, 201 feet on Jorale-
mon street, and 288 feet on Furman street, or nearly 800 feet in all.
The ground includes nearly twenty-four full-sized city lots, of which
the buildings cover less than half.

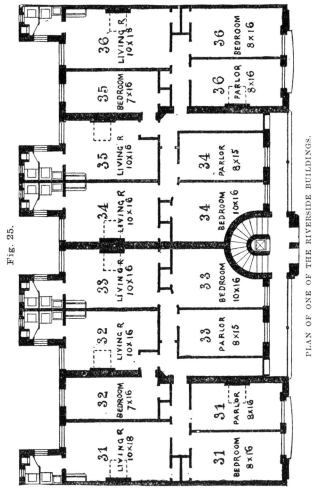

Fig. 25.

PLAN OF ONE OF THE RIVERSIDE BUILDINGS.

"The remainder of the area is left permanently open and is laid
out as a park for the use of the occupants of the Riverside.

"Apartments consist of sets of three, four, five and six rooms.
The majority of the sets are of four rooms, viz.: Living-room, par-

lor, bed-room and scullery; or living-room, two bed-rooms and scullery.

"The plans have been scientifically studied to give the maximum of health and comfort at the minimum of cost. They are intended to meet the wants of clerks, artisans, mechanics and all working-men and women who desire to live in private, pleasant homes, but can afford to pay only moderate rent.

"The rentals of apartments of three rooms, *i. e.*, living-room, bed-room and scullery, range from $1.50 to $2 per week, according to floor and location. The rentals of apartments of four rooms (*i. e.*, parlor, bed-room, living-room and scullery), range from $2 to $2.80 per week, according to floor, location and size of rooms. Apartments of five and six rooms from $2.70 to $4.

"The first aim has been to secure domestic privacy. Each apartment has its own front door opening into a small private hallway, from which all the rooms of the apartment are entered.

"The builings are only two rooms deep. instead of six rooms, as apartment houses are usually built. Every room is thus an ex-terior room, with a large window on the park or on the street, and each apartment controls a thorough ventilation from front to rear. There is also an abundant supply of water to each.

"A fire-proof staircase, most solidly built from cellar to roof, with easy ascent of slate steps, is set in a brick recess in front of the building, well lighted, well aired, and absolutely secured from danger in case of fire. The officials of the fire department con-sider these staircases the best possible safeguard, and the insurance companies show their appreciation by insuring these buildings at a far lower rate than ordinary structures.

"The open space in the centre of the buildings is about 255 feet in length by 115 feet in breadth. It is laid out with grass, trees, fountain and walks, as shown in the plan. At the south end a space of 50 by 80 feet is reserved as a children's play-ground, and is provided with swings, sand heaps, etc. In the centre of the park is a large shelter and music pavilion, where every Sunday, from May to November, from 4 to 6 P. M., a band furnishes music at the expense of the company.

"Provision has been made by the company for an adequate num-ber of bath-rooms, nicely fitted up, which are at the service of the tenants, free of charge, at certain hours daily. Lifts for coal, etc., are provided in all the buildings (with one exception, on Furman street.) The agent resides on the premises. Provision has been made in all these buildings for sixteen stores and four small shops. Stores rent from $25 upwards, and shops from $16 upwards per month. Each of the stores has a good cellar, with convenient access from the street. There are living-rooms in the rear of the stores and shops.

"When the first block of buildings was opened by this company every apartment was let in less than a week, and there are now on an average of ten applicants in advance for each vacancy that occurs in them."[1]

In New York the two largest enterprises of this kind are the Improved Dwellings Association and the Tenement-House Building Company.

The Improved Dwellings Association in 1882 erected a block of thirteen houses on the corner of East Seventy-second street and First avenue. Two hundred and eighty-five thousand dollars were expended in making them models of all that prior experience had found most useful. They can accommodate 218 families, in suites of from two to four rooms, at prices ranging from $6.25 for two rooms on the top floor to $14 for a suite of four rooms on the first floor. The buildings contain coal lifts, ash chutes, free baths and common laundries, and are built around a series of inner courts, which are cemented, and serve as a play-ground for the children.

By the terms of the stock the dividends are limited to 5 per cent. The association has had to meet a continual succession of unlooked for expenses, which have prevented a dividend of over 4 per cent., but this has been regularly paid. All surplus earnings have been expended upon the buildings, which have constantly increased in value.

---

[1] As unfortunately Mr. White's pamphlet describing his Brooklyn tenements is out of print, a list of other articles describing them is given for those interested.

New York Times, April 30, 1877. *New York Times,* November 5, 1877. *New York Evening Post,* May 5 and May 25, 1877. *New York Sun,* April 16, 1877. *New York Evening Mail,* May 28, 1877. *Sanitarian,* May, 1877. *Brooklyn Daily Eagle,* March 20, 1877.

Fig. 26.

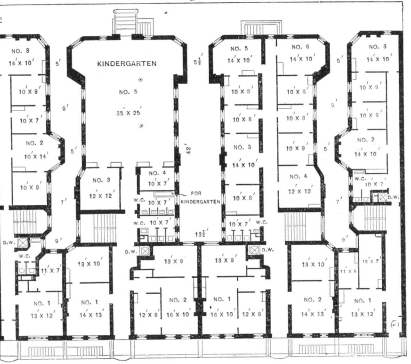

MODEL TENEMENT OF THE TENEMENT-HOUSE BUILDING COMPANY.

The Tenement-House Building Company opened on December 1, 1887, a block of six houses, Nos. 338 to 344 Cherry street, the plans of which are here given in Figure 28. The following description is taken from a publication of the company:[1]

"With a frontage of 116 feet 8 inches, they are six stories in height, with a basement throughout, and are arranged with large courts, varying in width from five feet to thirteen and one-half feet, so that every room opens to the outside, and has the advantage of ample light and air.

"The houses contain 108 apartments in two and three-room suites, but so arranged that they can be conveniently divided into

[1] "Tenement-houses of New York City."

suites of four, five or six rooms, to meet the requirements of large or small families. The two-room suites vary in rent from $7 to $9 a month, and the three-room suites from $10 to $14. There are 43 two-room and 61 three-room apartments, and four apartments besides occupied by a kindergarten. Wide entries running the length of the building, with large windows in the rear, opening on the outside, separate the rooms.

"The floors throughout are constructed in a manner which makes them practically fire-proof, and the first-story halls and all water-closets have iron beams and tile floors. . . . .

"The yards and basements are finished in granolithic, and are thoroughly drained and perfectly dry. In the basement separate storage closets for fuel and provisions are provided for each tenant.

" In the erection of these buildings the subjects of ventilation, lighting and sanitary plumbing have received special attention, the object being to avoid dark rooms and corners, to insure a thorough circulation of air through every room in the house, and, as far as possible, to expose each room to the sunlight during some part of the day. There is no room in the house without a window opening directly to the air. The entries are all provided with windows.

"The plumbing is of a superior order, and is arranged so that all piping, fittings and apparatus are exposed to view. Running water is provided on each floor. In one of the houses hot and cold water is supplied in each apartment, and in the other houses hot water is to be obtained in each basement, and cold water in each living-room.

" In the basement are laundries and bathrooms, with neat brick-faced walls and water-tight granolithic floors for the free use of the occupants. The baths are one of the most popular features of the apartments. There were originally four bath tubs in the basement, and this number has since been increased to nine. They are free to the tenants every day in the week at certain specified hours. There is scarcely an occupant who does not use them regularly. The common laundry in the basement is provided with hot and cold water. From the laundry the clothes can be sent up in the elevators and dried on the roof.

" The water closets are ample, one for each two apartments, and are constructed according to the most approved methods. In addition to an outside window, a large ventilating flue has been provided for each water closet, which insures a continuous circulation of air.

" The main hall, the kindergarten and the water closets are heated with steam from low pressure boilers, which are also used throughout the year for heating water for bathrooms, laundries and sinks.

"On the first floor of the houses is a large kindergarten. In this room, beside the kindergarten classes, sewing classes and small-boys' clubs also hold their meetings."

These advantages are shown in the death-rate, which is not only lower than the city's average death-rate, but is much lower than the death-rate in the tenement-houses erected since 1880. In 1888 (the date of the last census of the tenement-house population,) the general death-rate was 26.33 per thousand throughout the city, 23.06 in the old tenements, 22.42 in the new tenements, and only 14.28 in the company's houses. In 1889 and 1890 the company's houses show the same very low death-rate.

It is gratifying to note that the character of the neighborhood has much improved. A number of improved dwellings have been built and owners of property have been stimulated by the example of the company to erect a better class of tenements.

The large courts and wide entries reduce the rental capacity of the houses fully 30 per cent.

A large rental is usually earned from stores which occupy the first floor, but it is the fixed practice of the tenement-house company to refuse the use of its premises for store purposes. The company again manifests its interest in the welfare of its tenants by forbidding factory labor in its apartments. A part of the loss due to these rules is avoided, because in the "model houses," by reason of their healthfulness and the conveniences they offer to the tenants, the proportion of vacancies is smaller than in the ordinary tenement-house. While the average loss of rental through vacancies in ordinary tenements amounts to 10 per cent., in the building of the company the loss has been only about $5\frac{1}{2}$ per cent. The total loss from this source in 1890 was only \$731.83, with a total rental capacity of \$13,000. The proportion of evictions is also far below the average. During the year 1890 there were only six evictions. The repair and the cleaning of the apartments, made necessary by frequent changes in occupancy, are expenses which, therefore, bear less heavily on the model houses than on ordinary tenements.

The total cost of land and houses was \$152,715.13. The income (net) was, in 1889, $2\frac{3}{8}$ per cent.; in 1890, 4 per cent.; in 1891, $4\frac{3}{4}$ per cent. The dividends to the stockholders are limited to 4 per cent.

The surplus earnings are divided among the tenants in the manner described in the by-laws, as follows:[1]

"All the net earnings of the corporation, beyond the amount which may be necessary to pay declared dividends, shall be used as a reserve fund.

" The board of trustees shall, at their first meeting in each calendar year, apportion the reserve fund which may have been earned the preceding year among all persons who shall have been tenants during any part of that year, in proportion to the rent they have paid respectively, and shall credit to each person who shall have been a tenant during three-fourths of the whole year the share of such reserve fund which may have been apportioned to him on the books of the company.

"Any interest in the reserve fund credited to tenants shall be available only to be applied as rent for such tenants or their families at such times as they may request, and the board of trustees shall approve or as hereinafter provided; and the board of trustees shall approve such application in all cases where the tenant, by reason of illness, age, lack of employment, or other good causes, shall be unable to provide for the support of himself and family.

"Any tenant shall be entitled to purchase stock of the corporation and to have the purchase price thereof paid by the corporation from the amount credited to him on the books of the company, if such sum be sufficient."

As yet the company has been unable to divide a surplus income, for the first few years are always

---

[1] By-laws. Articles XVIII., XIX., XX. and XXIII.

costly, but the rate of increase has been constant, a small amount has yearly been added to the reserve fund, and it is thought that these provisions will in a short time be put in practice. The importance to the laborer of having a fund to fall back upon for his rent in case of misfortune or sickness, and a safeguard against the consequent eviction, cannot be overestimated.

The model tenements of both these companies contain kindergartens. The following from the report of the Cherry street kindergarten (October, 1890,) may be taken as applying to the others:

"The police of Boston and San Francisco testify to the fact that the entire character of vicious neighborhoods has been altered and improved by the presence of the kindergarten and the influence which emanates from it.

"The Cherry Street Kindergarten has become a centre from which healthful activities and good influences have radiated, and as such has played no unimportant part in the scheme organized by the association."

The use of the rooms is given free to a sewing class. The children in attendance range in years from six to fourteen. Most of them come from the model tenements, as do the members of the Boys' Club, who use the rooms also free of rent.[1]

The scheme long popular in Scotland, and lately introduced, with but scant success, by Sir Sydney Waterlow, of renting certain rooms in large tenements at a higher rate, until finally the tenant becomes actual owner of that part of the house, when he ceases to pay rent, has never, to my knowledge, been applied to tenant-houses in America. Sir Sydney Waterlow and others were most enthusiastic over the advantages of this method, and in 1881 had a law

---

[1] See *Harper's Weekly* of January 14, 1888.

7

passed entitled "The Chambers and Offices Act." This plan is thoroughly discussed by the Royal Commission on the Housing of the Working Classes.— "Evidence," page 422, and "Report," page 43.

While it is an excellent thing to encourage in the laborer the desire to own his residence, yet it is doubtful if he would think it worth his while to exercise the self-denial that the extra saving necessary for the higher rent would involve, for the sake of owning only a room in a building owned by another.

Two other examples, the best known in Boston, will sufficiently illustrate the model tenement companies. The Boston Co-operative Building Company was incorporated in 1871, and empowered "to hold and improve real estate in said city, as homes for working people at a moderate cost." Its assets, December 31, 1890, amounted to $310,969.29, on which a dividend was declared, January 15, 1891, of 6 per cent. $2,000 was added to the renewal fund, while there remained a balance, which was passed to one of the estates. These estates were reported to the board of health as being in an excellent sanitary condition, the death-rate being but 13.5 per 1,000.

The Improved Dwellings Association, of Boston, was incorporated in 1885, "For the purpose of erecting, maintaining, leasing and improving homes for working people and others of moderate means." The assets, as shown by the last report, were $119,-034.36, on which the net income was 5 per cent.

The property consists at present of the Broadway estate, comprising several stores and tenements, valued at $55,524, which clears 6 per cent. per annum, and the Second street estate, which cost $60,975, and brings in a net income of about 4½ per cent.   Here the company has been careful to admit only respectable tenants, and, as the neighborhood bears a poor reputation, it is difficult to keep the rooms well rented. It seems unwise to make any special effort to induce tenants to rent rooms in model tenements or prohibit any family from engaging them. All should have equal chances; but it should be well understood that disorderly habits will not be tolerated, and that they will be promptly followed by the removal of the offenders. The following description of the Second street buildings is compiled from the reports of the company for 1890 and 1891, while that of 1889 furnishes the plans here given.

In the spring of 1888 it was decided to try the experiment of building improved tenements in South Boston. The situation chosen was in a particularly bad, if not a dangerous, part of the city. The building known as the Rufus Ellis Memorial was fully completed about December 1, 1888. (The plans of this building are shown in Figs. 27 and 28.) The average rental per room per week in this section is 74 cents. More rent is charged in proportion for a single-room tenement than for tenements of two, three or four rooms. The total number of tenements is 56. The cost of land and buildings was about $61,000.

"The building has iron staircases, and layers of concrete in portions of the passage-ways, of the halls, and in the water-closets. The cellars are well lighted and spacious, and furnished with ample accommodations for coal and wood. Clothes are dried on the roof. Abundant fire-escapes are furnished. A janitor, with his wife and family, lives on the premises, and certain prescribed duties are required of him. The agent visits the buildings three times a week, collects the rents and exercises a general supervision.

"The building is situated between two streets, fronting on West Second, which is fifty feet wide. Every room has plenty of light and air. In the rear is a large playground, and up to the present

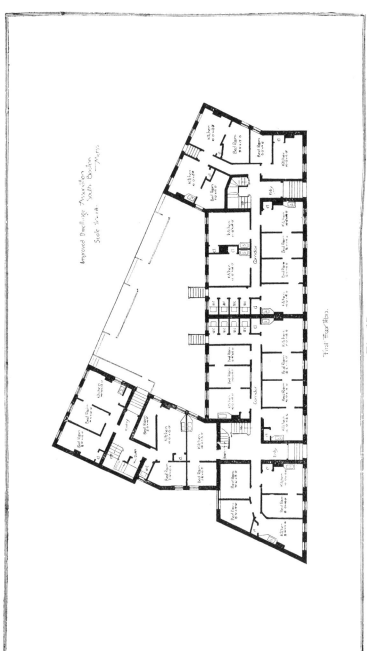

Fig. 27.

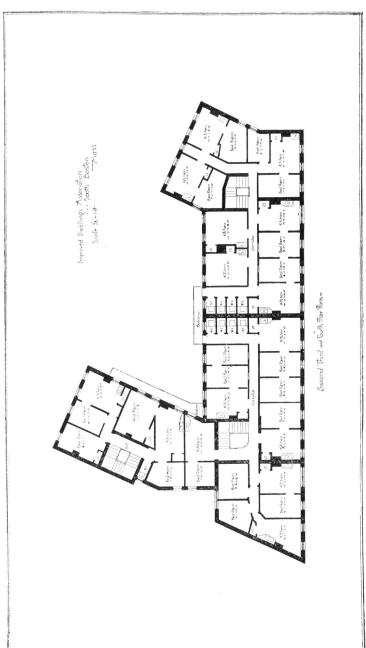

Fig. 28.

time a large space on one side of the building, belonging to the association, has been left open, on which children have been allowed to play.   If the building was fully occupied the net income would be about six per cent.   During the past year, with an average of seven vacancies, it has earned about 4½ per cent.   'The one-room tenants are the most popular,' says the agent, as they meet a need which is not elsewhere so well and so conveniently supplied.''

There has been erected in Brooklyn a most novel block of houses.   A plot of 112 feet on Baltic street and the same on Warren street, has been bought in the centre of the block, which is bounded on the two remaining sides by Henry and Hicks streets.   Through the centre of this plot runs a private way christened Warren Place, which is 24 feet wide, and had been laid out with a grass plot in the middle and flag walks on both sides, the whole being enclosed at either end by low iron fences.   On this front twenty-four two-story and basement houses, while on Warren and Baltic streets front eight large houses.   In the rear of the houses run cartways for ash-carts, delivery wagons, etc.

The houses fronting on Warren Place are each 11½ feet wide and 32 feet deep.   These have six rooms, each with a good closet.   The staircase rises with a half turn in the centre of the house. The front basement is the dining-room, and the rear basement the kitchen, which is furnished with a good range, boiler, sink, washtub, dresser and coal closet.   A rear door from the kitchen leads into a small lobby, opening on the cartway already mentioned.   From this lobby another door opens into the water-closet, which is thus disconnected from the house, though under the same roof.   The first and second floors have each two rooms, that is, one parlor and three bed-rooms in all.   The end houses are one story higher, and

contain nine rooms. The fronts of all are planned
with slightly projecting doorways, trimmed with
slate and bluestone, and under the windows are slate
flower sills with ornamental guards.[1]

The cost of the six-room houses is a little under
$1,100 each. With a little crowding 32 houses of
six rooms could be put upon a plot 100x200, or eight
city lots. Taking $1,500 as a basis of cost for
such houses when ten or more are built at a
time, and assuming that a gross rental of 12 per
cent. per annum, or one per cent. per month, will
surely yield 7 per cent. net, it is easy to figure what
rentals could be afforded in upper New York. On
ground costing even $4,000 per lot of 25x100 feet, the
cost of land for each house would be, say $1,000; add
$1,100 for building, and we have cost of houses and
lots $2,100, on which one per cent. per month makes
a monthly rental of only $21. With land at $2,000
per lot, rentals could be brought down to $16 per
month, and, in the suburbs, land at $800 per lot
would reduce the monthly rental to $13. Such a
house is not palatial in any respect, but it certainly
does afford all that is needed, even by a good-sized
family. In six rooms any ordinary family can live
decently, and a little added to the cost of each
house would make them suited to any neighborhood.
The owners of these houses aimed, in this building
enterprise, to erect the best six-room houses possible
to be substantial, convenient, healthy and attractive, for a cost of about $1,000. Their buildings
establish beyond dispute the feasibility of erecting
this class of houses, not only in Brooklyn, but in
New York. Plots can be had which might be covered

---

[1]See *Harper's Magazine*, of April, 1884.

with small houses rented at $25 or $30 per month, with equal profits to landlords and tenants. In ten years, should the land become valuable, these little houses could be torn down, and yet the land owners would be wealthier for having built them than if the land were left idle to consume itself in taxes.

These houses are intended for the highest class of workmen, who now compete with families of less means for the best rooms in the tenements. Remove them from the competition by erecting large numbers of houses like these in districts such as upper New York, where the blocks are badly arranged, and the entire tenement population would be advanced a stage, all being thus benefitted. Unfortunately these homes, small as they are, must rent in our largest cities for about $17, while only the better class of workmen can afford to pay over $13 a month rent. That these houses are far above even the best model tenement in the moral advantages which result from giving each family its own front door, its own halls, and, indeed, its own house, is indisputable. How, then, may rent be reduced?

As has been stated, thirty-two houses can be put upon eight city lots. At $2,500 a lot the ground would cost $20,000, while the cost of the houses at $1,100 a house is $35,000. Now it seems to me that as these houses are but two stories high, two or three additional stories could be built above them, (but with no connection with the houses below,) having an entrance by a staircase in an external tower, and having access either from the street or from the wagon way in the rear. These additional floors could be divided into houses on a plan similar to that of the

stories below. The staircase could be carried up to
the first floor of this second tier of houses, where
galleries could lead off to right and left, one staircase giving access to four or more "houses," while
each house in this second tier has its own interior
staircase leading up to the upper stories. Or the
common staircase could be carried to the top and
each floor divided on a plan similar to the model
tenements, with no more reference to the floors
below than the supporting cross walls would necessitate. The first method seems to me to be the more
advisable, as it prevents the tenement aspect and
atmosphere, which might attach to the blocks, if the
upper floors were divided on a tenement-house plan.
This scheme seems to me to have many advantages,
chief of which is the decreased expense; for the cost
of the land, ($20,000), the foundations, roofs, ex-
penses for supervision, the cost and care of the central plot and the rear wagon ways and the many
other things would thus be divided, while the whole
block, being on twice as large a scale, the cost of
building and plumbing would be materially lessened.
The block of 68 houses could be erected at a cost
under $65,000, which, with the land at $20,000,
would make the total $85,000; 12 per cent. gross
rental would certainly yield 7 per cent. net, which,
on $85,000 is $10,200, and this, among the 64 houses,
is only $13.25 for a month's rent, a sum well within
the reach of the better class of laborers.

The Beneficent Building Association of Philadelphia (capital $52,300) has lately erected some single
houses $13\frac{1}{2}$ x 16 feet, three stories high, consisting of
three rooms, one over another, with a "hanging bath-

room" extension, a novelty in small-house construction. These are rented for $12 a month.

In London, The Artizans, Laborers, and General Dwellings' Company, Limited, owning three large estates, has built about 4,000 houses. This company furnishes eight-room houses on plots 16 x 85, for twelve shillings per week, six-room houses on plots 15 x 70, for ten shillings; five room houses, eight shillings; and on plots 13 x 60, four-room houses for six to seven shillings, weekly. Their net income was in 1882 over £50,000, paying five per cent. per annum on the stock £955,000.

It has been suggested that manufacturers provide their employees with rooms in model tenements, erected by themselves. Messrs. Cross & Blackwell have done this in England, and find that it is profitable, for five per cent. can be obtained on their money; while their employees, if properly housed and fed, are much more efficient workmen. Interest in the welfare of the company also, which is mutually beneficial, is created. The same experiment has been tried in many of our smaller manufacturing cities, such as Lowell, Mass., with good success. City governments might lead the way by building tenements for the many laborers employed on their public works. This was tried by a city in Scotland, Glasgow, if I remember rightly, but with signally poor results, and its policy would be doubtful here, for it might not be wise to discourage the healthy competition of private builders.

Unhealthy, crowded tenements will always house the poor of our towns until private enterprise has provided something better at the same or lower rent. When these are provided they will be well patronized, as they have been in every case, and the poorer houses will have to come up to the standard set by them or remain empty from lack of patronage. Private enterprise will embark on such an investment if it is clearly demonstrated that a dividend of at'least five per cent. will be forthcoming. It is difficult to persuade owners of the old class of tenements that better houses can be provided for the same class of tenants and yet yield a good return.

The Peabody fund, The Improved Industrial Dwellings and other companies in England, the Improved Dwellings Company of Brooklyn, the Tenement House Building Company and the Improved Dwelling Association in New York, the Beneficent Building Association and the many houses erected in Philadelphia by Mr. Theodore Starr, all offer a practical demonstration that "Philanthropy and five per cent." represents an accomplished fact. It must be well understood that the success of these companies is due to their strict observance of business principles. There should be nothing in the management of such buildings which savors of charity in any way, or the better class of tenants will be driven away, and those who remain will do so at the cost of self-respect. Fair rents, not charity, is what the workingman requires. Another evil is pointed out by Mr. White.

"Fair return for fair rents, simple justice, and not that which is falsely called charity, is what the industrious laboring classes ask, and what they are entitled to. It is, moreover, unfair to wage a ruinous competition with landlords who may be striving to give the laboring classes good homes for their money, but who need a fair interest on their investment; the manifest result should be to discourage and arrest the erection of improved buildings, instead of encouraging real estate owners and builders to aid in the needed reform. To make the example accomplish any great good, it must be shown that it is to the interest of capitalists to follow it.

"The *London Telegraph* says:

" 'Offer the workmen the opportunity of buying that to which he has a just claim, at a fair price, without being held under any obligation or asked for thanks. Any other plan simply converts a block of workmen's dwellings into thinly disguised pauper barracks.'

"To those who intend to erect improved dwellings for workingmen the following hints may be of service:

Location.—Choose a district where tenement houses are being built by speculative builders; these watch the drift of population closely. You can afford to pay as much for land as they can, and high cost is no detriment, provided the value is made by the pressure of people seeking residence there. Choose preferably the border land of the tenement district to the heart of it, unless your undertaking is a very large one.

Size of Plot.—The larger the plot the better, for a large plot allows superior arrangements for light, air and play-grounds, and also permits the employment of the whole time of a competent man or woman as agent and superintendent of the buildings.

Accommodations.—Three rooms and a scullery are the accommodations sought by most workingmen; but two rooms and a scullery suffice for small families of two or three people. Learn what rents are paid by the average workingman in the locality selected, and plan the building so that your rents average the same, giving the tenant as many conveniences as this average rental will allow, while returning a fair interest on the investment. In determining this it is well to remember that the governing considerations should be: first, domestic privacy, the foundation of morality; second, sanitary conditions, the mainspring of health; third, comfort, convenience, attractiveness."[1]

VIII.

Cottages in the Suburbs—Unwillingness of Workmen to Live Far from their Work—Objections and Advantages.

The methods already discussed improve the homes of the workingman, but they do not lift him from the tenement. At best they provide him with better rooms and better air, but they are tenement rooms

---

[1] "Better Homes for Workingmen." By Alfred T. White.

and tenement air for all that. A cottage in the
suburbs is certainly more attractive, and where this
method is practicable, far better results are reached
than by any of the others.

Unfortunately the peculiar location of many of our
cities prohibits this solution of the problem. The
restricted limits of New York, for instance, will
probably always be an insurmountable obstacle to
providing homes for the workingman in its vicinity.
Here the confident belief expressed in the report of
the board of health of 1874, that rapid transit would
solve the difficulty has been seen to be a vain hope.
The hour lost in going and coming to his work more
than counterbalances the advantages gained by
suburban residence, in the mind of the average
workman.

At whatever cost of comfort and health, and even
of money, the workman will live near his work, and
unless the factories are moved into the suburbs,
he will continue to reside in the most crowded
portion of our cities. He is unwilling also to ex-
change the pleasures and bustle of the city for the
comparative quiet of the suburbs. A small portion,
however, the better class, would everywhere gladly
embrace the opportunity were it offered. The experiment was tried a short time in London. The
Great Eastern Railway, in consideration of certain
privileges, sold at one shilling tickets good for a
week, to those workmen who lived in the suburbs. Great trouble was experienced by the road,
for, if allowed in the regular cars, they were objectionable to the other patrons of the road. About
7,000 daily availed themselves of the privilege. The
road was finally forced to appeal and in the inquiry

which resulted, testimony was given showing that special trains could not be given at a less rate than two shillings a head, a price above the means of even the higher class of workmen.

A syndicate has lately (1891) been formed in New York with a capital of $400,000, which intends to purchase about thirty acres in the twenty-third and twenty-fourth wards, and erect thereon a hundred frame dwellings of the kind known as three-thousand five-hundred-dollar houses, to be purchased on the instalment plan. Unfortunately these houses will be far beyond the means of all but the highest class of workmen, but the others will be indirectly benefited by decreasing the competition.

Philadelphia, the city of homes, may well be compared with New York to show the success that may attend this method.

In June, 1890, 50.18 per cent. of all the dwellings in New York city were occupied by less than ten persons each, while 49.82 per cent. contained more than ten persons each.

Of the entire population 250,002 persons, or 16.50 per cent. only, occupied dwellings containing less than ten persons each, while 1,265,299 persons, or 83.50 per cent. of the entire population, lived in houses containing more than ten persons each. No less than 1,010,786, or 66.70 per cent. of the entire population, live in houses which are occupied by more than twenty persons each.

In Philadelphia, at the same time, out of a total of 187,052 dwellings, more than twice the number in New York, 95.61 per cent. contain ten persons or less each, and 8,213, or 4.39 per cent. only, more than ten persons each. Out of a population of 1,046,964 persons, 913,076, or 87.21 per cent., live in dwellings containing less than ten persons each, and but 12.79 per cent. or 133,888 persons in dwellings containing more than ten persons each.

In Philadelphia 84.64 per cent. of the total number of families occupy dwellings by themselves, while in New York but 12.02 per cent. are thus accommodated.

Dwellings with three or more families each are generally considered as tenement houses. In New York 42.77 per cent. of all the families lived in houses of this class, while in Philadelphia only 1.44 per cent. of the total number of families lived in such houses.

Philadelphia covers over 82,560 acres, Manhattan Island has an area of 12,673 acres.

The death-rate in Philadelphia was in 1889, 19.7; in New York city 25.19. The success of this method in Philadelphia has been due largely to the many coöperative societies, which are more popular there than in any other city. As coöperation is most intimately connected with this method of housing our working classes, a short review of its history, methods and success may not be out of place.

Coöperative building associations were introduced in Philadelphia in 1831; in 1874 the number had increased to 400; at present there are about 500 in that city alone. The New Jersey labor bureau a number of years ago estimated the number of building associations in the United States at 3,000, with 450,000 members and $75,000,000 capital. They provide for the investment of $300,000,000 at any given time. A later authority places the number of such associations at 4,580. The following account of the process by which a workingman can accumulate money enough to erect and finally to own his house, is condensed from several articles on this subject and from the latest reports of a number of coöperative banks, nearly all of which publish annual reports and copies of the state laws, which may be had on application.

Shares of stock are issued to members of the association, upon which they make weekly or monthly payments, termed dues, until the sums paid, increased from the dividends added to them, reach a certain sum, called the matured value of the stock. This money is loaned only to share-holders, and in sums corresponding to the matured value of a share or a multiple thereof, and each stockholder who can give the requisite security has an equal right with every other stockholder to borrow the money of the association.   No stockholder can borrow a sum exceeding the matured value of the shares held by him, and the money is offered to those desiring to borrow at stated weekly or monthly meetings.   In all cases where there is a competition for the loan the right to the same is determined by the bidding of a premium, and is awarded to the highest bidder.   In some associations a minimum premium is required.   The premium bid may be a certain sum per share, which is deducted from the loan when the security is given, this being called the " gross plan."   Or it may be a certain sum per share, to be paid in weekly or monthly instalments, with interest upon the loan and the dues upon the stock.   This is called the "instalment plan."   Or it may be a bidding upon the rate of interest to be paid upon the loan.   This is called the interest premium plan.   Interest in all cases must be paid weekly or monthly, at the same time that the

dues are paid.   The security required is a bond secured by first mortgage upon unencumbered real
estate or pledge of the stock of the association.
There are a great many variations in the detail of
this general outline among different associations.

The gross profits of the association will consist of
interest, premiums, shares of profits left by with-
drawing shareholders, fines, transfer and entrance
fees.

From each monthly payment the portion called
dues is at once credited towards the debt.   All these
credits form a sinking fund for the eventual liquida-
tion of the debt.

In Philadelphia a small house and lot may be had
for $1,000. The great number of householders testifies
to the success of this method.

In England coöperative building associations have
been as successful as they have been in this country.
There is such an abundance of literature on this subject that it is unnecessary to discuss it further here.
In the bibliography a few of the best American
authors are given.   No reference is, however, made
to the many valuable books and reports published in
England.

The Windsor Royal and the Prince Albert societies
in England have erected a large number of cheap
but attractive cottages in the suburbs of London.
They have met with very fair success in keeping
them well filled and the rents moderate.

A generation ago the English public was as much
aroused over the reform of the laborer's cottage as
it was nearly ten years ago over the tenements.   As
a result, the evils have greatly decreased, and a large
amount of literature on the best plan of the laborer's

8

cottage was produced, a portion of which (to be found for the most part in the current English magazines), is applicable to America to-day.

The Society of Arts offered prizes for the best plans of such a cottage and published a book comprising plans, sections, elevation details and estimates of the two best designs. The houses of the poor in the suburbs of our cities are too well known to need description. For books containing good plans and estimates of this class of houses see the bibliography.

The advantages of providing our poor with cheap homes in the suburbs are self-evident, but in many towns this will always be an impossibility, while in all cities a very large number will always be unwilling or unable to avail themselves of this method for their relief. A great though indirect benefit to them, however, will be the relief afforded by the decrease in pressure which will result from the removal of the more well-to-do from the competition for homes in the city.

IX.

THE BOARDING-TENEMENT AND THE LODGING-HOUSE.

The various methods which have been already discussed are, each in its way, of much benefit to the greater part of the working classes, but there are those in all of our large cities who are helped very little by any of them.

It is this class that General Booth denominates the "submerged tenth." These are they who are not reached by the model tenement, because even the lowest rents are beyond their means. In America,

happily, their number is less than abroad, where
even the buildings of the Peabody fund are beyond
the reach of thousands; yet even here it is considerable, while the evil influence exercised by them is
very powerful in corrupting others.

The more well-to-do, if such a term can be used
without sarcasm, rent a single room which suffices
for the entire family, and there is room enough for
one or two boarders besides.   The second class is
constituted by the boarders themselves, who pay
about 70 cents a week for the privilege of sharing
the apartment, or, when they also eat with the
family, from $2 to $3 for both board and lodging.
The third class consists mostly of men out of work,
or strangers in the city, who put up at the cheap
lodging-houses, while the remainder of the "tenth"
make no pretensions of having a home, but sleep
where and when they can.

The first of these classes, when the cause of their
unfortunate surroundings is want, and not a desire
to save, as is often the case, are almost beyond any
help but charity. The causes of poverty are many,
but the most important are lack of work and the high
prices which must be paid for the necessaries of life,
when bought in small quantities.   The latter are
usually purchased from the little retail stores in the
basements of the poorer tenements, hundreds of which
may be found in any district wholly peopled by the
poor.   These little shops exercise a far greater influence upon the condition of the poor than would
appear at first sight.

I would again call attention to the fact that in the
United States the income of a workingman is found

to be divided among the various items of expenditure in the following ratio:

Subsistence	45.33	per cent.
Clothing	18.47	"
Rent	18.58	"
Fuel	4.97	"
Sundries	12.65	"
Total	100.00	"

It is not too much to say that of the total income 95 per cent. is expended within a radius of a few blocks from the home of the family.

The supplies of all kinds which are classified under the head of subsistence come from little stores in the immediate vicinity. From here also come the fuel, much of the clothing and a large proportion of the sundries. The rest of the clothing comes from the cheap clothing stores in the neighborhood.

Placing aside the amount expended for rent, for clothing, and half the amount spent for sundries, we find that fully 57 per cent. of the yearly income is expended in these little retail stores. It is important, therefore, to consider whether this large amount is profitably spent, whether the prices asked are reasonable, and the goods of fair quality.

All these stores do a strictly cash business from necessity. Families move so frequently in the tenement-house district that were credit given money would certainly be lost. Rate wars are frequently carried on, to the great interest of the customers, but are of short duration, because the capital on which the places are carried on is too small to stand the loss of profit involved for more than a few days.

It is hard to believe that it costs the poor, who patronize these little stores, more for the necessaries of life than the wealthiest persons pay at the best shops, and yet it is true.

The fact is that these stores are in reality middlemen between the regular retailers and the people of the tenement, whose small means will not allow them to purchase their necessaries in the quantities sold by retailers.   The housewife of a tenement family expends but thirty or forty cents on the supplies for the day.   With that amount she purchases meat, vegetables, flour or bread, a few coals and a small bundle of wood.   Two or three cents are expended for one article, five cents for another.   Commodities elsewhere bought by the pound are here purchased by the ounce; coal and wood, instead of being bought by the wagon load, are bought almost by the piece.   The prices have to be high, for selling in such small quantities they have to purchase in small quantities.   Even though capital were at their command, they would be prevented by the very smallness of the store from buying in large quantities.   Owing to these facts their wholesales prices are nearly as high as are the usual retail prices.

Like limitations prevent the purchasers from buying in large quantities.   They have but a limited amount of money at their disposal, they cannot buy a barrel or even a bag of flour, for if they did they would be without other provisions.   They do not want a pound of butter or a leg of meat, for they have no ice to keep it on.   Nor can they buy large quantities of coal or wood, for they have no place in which to store it, even though they had the money with which to buy it.   Let us now examine the actual prices paid by the poor for the necessaries of life when purchased at these stores.   A barrel of flour is expected to bring in about $10, for it is sold at the rate of 5 cents a pound. The same quality can be bought for about $5 a barrel elsewhere. Butter, bought by the quarter of a pound at a time, brings from 32 to 40 cents a pound; elsewhere it may be obtained for from 25 to 30 cents a pound, or for very much less if bought by the tub. Washing soda, which may be obtained elsewhere at 3 cents a pound, sells for 1 cent an ounce. Sugar is 3 cents a cup, or about 7 cents a pound, while cheap teas sell for 40 cents a pound and inferior coffee at 30 cents.

Coal is sold at 14 cents a pail, and enough pails can be filled from a ton to bring in a return of $14 on the $5 invested. The profits on the sale of wood are in like proportion.

It must not be thought that these stores are patronized exclusively by the very poor. They furnish the supplies to nearly all of the residents of the neighborhood, many of whom are hard-working persons, neither ignorant nor improvident. They patronize these places because it is convenient to do so, and because they must purchase in small quantities since their means and the lack of space prevent them from doing otherwise. As long as they are compelled to purchase by the ounce and pound articles which are usually bought by the pound and ton, so long will they pay extravagant prices.

As we have seen, 57 per cent. of the total expenditure of a workingman's family is spent in these small stores, where the poor are fortunate if they get half value for their money. Would it not be well to devise some means by which this needless expenditure could be prevented so that a greater amount might be expended upon the home and the cultivation of that home-life which is more important than the small proportion expended for rent would indicate?

With such prices to pay for the necessaries of life, it is little wonder that the poor seldom lift themselves to better circumstances. Coöperative stores have been tried as a remedy for this evil. Another, as yet not suggested, I believe, by any one else, I propose to offer as possibly efficacious in reaching that class which is beyond all relief save that of charity.

The cause of most of this misfortune of the very poor is that wages alone will not meet the expenses. The result is that the family must be crowded into a space too small for it, boarders must be taken, or the room let for purposes which make it unhealthy, and the daily provisions must be bought in such small quantities as to necessitate the spending of about twice the normal amount. How, then, can more revenue be brought in and the expenses at the same time be reduced?

I would build a model tenement on the general plan of those already considered, but supplied with an additional number of lifts. A portion of the basement or attic I would fit up as a large and well-appointed kitchen. This should be put under the supervision of a competent house-keeper, and a requisite number of cooks, capable of cooking the simple kinds of food, such as bread, meat, vegetables, etc., must be under her orders. Each family should be furnished with a printed list giving the prices for which the various articles of food, prepared for the table, will be supplied. This can be changed as the market prices change. Printed blanks will also be furnished which the woman of the family will fill out with the various articles, and the amounts which she will require for the following day. They are to be left with the house-keeper, who will make her purchases accordingly. The amount of each kind of food required by all the tenants will be cooked in the company's kitchen by the company's servants (who may be obtained from among the tenants themselves), and will be sent up the lifts to the respective rooms. A deposit may be required in advance or a cash payment may be insisted on.

The greater economy and healthfulness of this method are so striking that it is strange that it has never been put into practice. The economy is twofold. In the first place the immense and useless expenditure instanced above, in buying food in small quantities at exorbitant rates, will be saved, while the food being bought at wholesale prices can be furnished at a fair price and yet yield a good profit, which is derived, not from the tenants, but from the especially advantageous prices of purchase.

A much smaller amount of food need be purchased, as in large quantities a great amount of waste is saved, while the food will cook to better advantage. The expense of fuel and a stove will be saved to the tenants, as well as the rent of a kitchen or living-room. The rooms could also be heated economically by the company in connection with the kitchen fires. Clothes could be washed and ironed in a common room as is now done in many of the model tenements. In the second place, the women of the family can add to the revenue by spending the time in work, which would otherwise be spent over the stove. A certain number would also be ensured a situation in the kitchen. The advantage from a sanitary standpoint would also be immense. The food would be of a much better quality. It would be cooked in a better way, and the tenants would feel that they could afford the necessary amount since they were buying to the best advantage. The gain to the healthfulness of the atmosphere of the whole building by removing the many kitchens, with their foul steam and odors of cooking and washing, would be great, while the gain in comfort and health to the individual rooms by their removal would be incalculable. I have been in many a kitchen in even the better tenements, where the smell on entering was intolerable, while the air, heavy with the combined odors of cooking, washing, and kerosene stoves, spoke volumes in support of the statement of a New York physician that one-half of the lung troubles of the populations of our cities are due to this cause. It must be remembered that these kitchens are the living-rooms of the entire family and that in them is spent the whole day of the younger children. Ask any of the summer physicians of our sanitary boards, and he will bear witness to the terrible sufferings of the poor in summer from the stove, whose heat reaches to every side of the small rooms. The charge to the tenants for heat, better food and better rooms than they are at present enjoying could, thanks to the savings which always result from doing things on a large scale, be brought well within the amount which they now pay for these accommodations. It would probably be impracticable to provide a common table for the tenants, but it seems to me that some such a scheme as has been outlined above would be of the greatest use in relieving the wants of the very poor, on a business-like, not charitable, basis.

There are certain houses, which offer themselves as temporary homes to others of the very poor, which need a most careful surveillance. I refer to the cheap lodging-houses. They were started in New York in 1877, but so profitable were they that in 1889 there were 345 houses which offered a night's lodging at from 5 to 25 cents. The report of the police department for the year ending December 31, 1888, states that in New York city the enormous number of 4,649,660 cheap lodgings were furnished during the year by 267 houses, containing 10,439 rooms. If tenement life tends to immorality and vice, certainly the 58 lodging-houses in the eleventh precinct, which furnished 1,243,200 lodgings in one year, must have the same or a worse tendency. In this year 150,812 lodgings were furnished at the station-house, making the total number of lodgings 4,800,472. The police report of the following year shows that the number of lodgings furnished by such houses had increased to 4,974,025, which, with those furnished by the station-houses, make the total of 5,121,659, an average of 14,000 for every night in the year. The rate of increase has been nearly the same for the last four years.

The character of these lodging-houses has been strongly drawn by Superintendent Byrnes, who states that it is an undeniable fact that the lodging-houses of the city have a powerful influence in producing, fostering and increasing crime, since they have come to be very largely frequented by thieves and criminals of the lowest class. In searching for a cheap lodging place, the young man, stranded in the great city, naturally drifts into these places, and is corrupted by the criminals or paupers who frequent them.

The only way which Mr. Byrnes sees open to re-form this evil lies through legislation. "There should be stringent laws enacted by the legislature for the regulation of lodging-houses. * * * The records and books should be open to the inspection of the proper authorities. It should be made a misdemeanor for the proprietor to mutilate or destroy his books, and he should be compelled to keep an accurate record of all his lodgers. No person, not of good character, should be allowed to be the proprietor of such a lodging-house, while the number of his lodg-ers should be proportional to the size of the rooms."

There is need for the model lodging-house as well as the model tenement. That it would be a profitable as well as a philanthropic investment is assured by the multitude, five million strong, who yearly make these lodgings their temporary homes. Several have lately been started in New York city, but there is room for many more.

One cause of much of the misery in our tenements has escaped attention, possibly because we have con-cerned ourselves so much with the tenement districts, that we have not thought of looking to the fashion-able quarters of the town. I refer to the careless or absent landlord. When the health board of New York investigated the question, it reported that inquiry often disclosed the fact that the owner of the property was a wealthy gentleman or lady, either living in an aristocratic part of the city or in a neigh-boring city, or, as was occasionally found to be the case, in Europe. The property is usually managed entirely by an agent, whose instructions are simple but emphatic: "Collect the rent in advance, or fail-ing, eject the occupants." Happily, this is not now as true as it was in those days, but still more true than is generally supposed. If a few of these absentee landlords could be compelled to keep their property in a sanitary condition, it would have a most salutary effect and save the various boards of health much trouble. Many of the owners, indeed the greater part, are ignorant of the condition of their property, which they in many cases have sublet. They would be the last persons to countenance the evil if they realized their own responsibility. If the owners of all tenements containing more than a certain number of occupants could be compelled to keep a housekeeper or agent on the premises, who should be held strictly responsible to the board of health, much good would result and the surveillance of the houses would be greatly simplified. Experience has shown that this would be far from a burden upon the owners. The houses where the owner or agent lives are always the most orderly; there is less damage to the property and the responsibility for it is more easily fixed. The responsibility of those who are possessed of wealth for the evils of the wretched tenement, is also evident.

Builders will always try to evade the spirit of the law until they discover that it is unprofitable to erect tenements of this character. These will continue to be well patronized until a sufficient number of model tenements have been built to produce a new and higher standard.

Millions of dollars are yearly given in America to charities and educational institutions of every kind. It seems strange that it is difficult to induce the wealthy to *invest, not give,* enough money to build a sufficient number of model tenements. Experience has shown that a higher rate of interest will be returned than if it were invested in government bonds. The formation of numerous building companies with purchasable stock will, by uniting many small amounts, show the profit and safety of the investment. When this is clearly demonstrated there will be no difficulty in raising the requisite amount.

To summarize: The highest grade of our working classes should be removed from the competition for the best rooms of the tenements by providing cheap, but independent houses in the suburbs when practicable, or in the city, in houses built on the general plan of the Warren Place houses, herein described. For the less well-to-do the model tenements will provide a home. Those whose revenues are too limited to allow them to maintain a kitchen and suite of rooms, could still afford to live, and live well, in the "boarding tenements," as has been suggested. The homeless poor might find accommodations in model lodging houses. Legislation must pass and enforce the observance of the requisite sanitary laws, and should compel, in certain cases, a resident agent and hold him responsible for the tenement over which he is placed. It should force the owners to alter existing tenements in compliance with certain requirements, and prevent the erection of others, unless on an approved type. The worst plague spots, like Mulberry Bend, in New York, might be cleared by expropriation, but the greatest care should be exercised against any needless interference with the laws of supply and demand.

Personal influence alone can affect the very lowest class of the poor who are indifferent to their surroundings and have little or no desire to improve. Both landlords and tenants must be educated to a better understanding of their rights and responsibilities. Little, however, can be accomplished until public interest is aroused, which will assist all reasonable attempts to lift the workingman above his present surroundings and create for him the healthful influences of home life.

BIBLIOGRAPHY.

TENEMENT HOUSE LIFE AND POPULATION.

Association for Improving the Condition of the Poor. Report 1877–8. New York.

Bitter Cry of Outcast London. Rev. Mearns.

Board of Health. Report for 1866. New York.

Board of Health. Report for 1874. New York.

Board of Health. Report for 1891. New York.

City Slums. J. A. Ingham. London, Swan, Sonnenschein & Co.

Condition of the Bristol Poor. Report of the Commission to Inquire into the. P. S. King & Sons. London, 1 vol., 1884.

Council of Hygiene and Public Health to the Citizens' Association. Report of. New York, January, 1864.

Das Arbeiter-Quartier in Mülhausen und Elsass. Mart. Schall. Berlin, 1877.

Zur Reform der Wohnungszustände in grossen städten. Mathias G. Ratkowsky. Wien, 1871.

Dwellings and Families in 1890. Extra *Census Bulletin* No. 19.

Dwellings of the People. Mansion House Council on the. 14 Clements Inn, Strand, London.

Dwellings of the Poor. Report of the Charities Organization Society. 1881.

Dwellings of the Poor. S. Loch. 1882.

Dwellings of the Poor. George Howell. *Nineteenth Century*, June, 1883.

Dwellings of the Poor. H. O. Arnold. *Nineteenth Century*, December, 1883.

Dwellings of the Poor. Series of articles in *Scribner's Magazine* for 1892.

Etudes sur les effects et les causes des logements insalubres. Dr. Marjolin. 1881.

Habitation des pauvres à Paris. du Mesnil. 1882.

Homes for the People. R. I. Paine. *Journal of Social Science*, No. XV. 1881.

Homes of the Poor. Scloss. 1885.

Horrible London. George R. Sims.

How the Other Half Lives. Jacob A. Riis.

How the Poor Live. George R. Sims. 1883.

Logements insalubres. Emile Laurent.

Logements insalubres de la ville de Paris. 1878–1883.

Rapport général sur les travaux de la commission. Dr. Du Mesnil. 1884.

Maisons salubres et insalubres. L. Masson et Dr. A. J. Martin. 1885. Paris.

Misères et Remèdes. Comte d'Haussonville. 1886.

Mortality of Tenement Houses. Report by the Registrar of Vital Statistics. 1888.

Outcast London. Rev. Andrew Mearns. *Contemporary Review*, December, 1883.

Outcast Poor. Brooke Lambert. *Contemporary Review*, December, 1883.

Overcrowding. Evidence before Commission of Enquiry. England. 1882.

Tenement Life. *Pall Mall Gazette*, November, 1883.

Populations urbaines en France comparées à celles de l'étranger. M. E. Levasseur. Published by Picard. 1887.

Situation des classes ouvrieres. Rapport fait au nom de la Commission. Le Comte de Melun. 1875.

Question des habitations ouvrieres en France et a l'étranger.

La situation actuelle, ses dangers et ses remèdes. G. Masson. 1886.

Sanitary Aid Society. Report for 1887. New York.

Sanitary Condition of Tenement Houses. Report of the Bureau of Statistics of Labor (Mass., New York, Conn., and New Jersey).

Sociale Fragen. Victor-Aime Huber.

Society's Exiles, by B. O. Fowler. (Tenements of Boston.) *Arena*, June, 1891.

State Charities Aid Association. The State Charities Record for 1884. New York.

Census of Tenement-houses in New York in 1867.

Tenement-house Commission. Report of select committee to examine the condition of tenement-houses in New York City made to the Legislature in March, 1857.

Tenement-houses and their Population. L. M. Hall. M. D. *Journal of Social Science*, 1885.

Tenement house Commission. (New York State.) Report 1884.

Tenements of New York described by C. F. Wingate in the *New York Tribune* (Nov. 23, 1884, and six following Sunday editions).

Tenement-house System in New York. Report by Dr. R. H. Derby, to the New York State Charities Aid Associations, February 23. 1879.

Wohnungsnoth der ärmeren Klassen in den deutschen Grosstädten. 1886.

Wohnungsverhältnisse unserer ärmeren Klassen. 1886.

Wohnungszustände der Arbeiter Classen. Emil Sai. Wien, 1869.

Causes of the Increase of Crime. Testimony of the Secretary of the Prison Association of New York, before a Legislative Committee, 1865.

Conference of Charities and Correction. Report of the XVI Conference, Omaha, 1889.

Great Cities and Social Reform. Samuel H. Barnett. *Nineteenth Century*, November, 1883.

Jukes, The. R. L. Dugdale. Putnam, N. Y. 1888.

Nurseries of Crime. Inspector Byrnes. *North American Review*, September, 1889.

Pauperism in the United States. Professor Richard T. Ely. *North American Review*, April, 1891.

Problems of a Great City. Arnold White. London, Remington Co.

Promotion of Social Purity. M. A. Brinkman. *North American Review*, April, 1891.

Workman's Reflections. William Glazier. *Nineteenth Century*, December, 1883.

Workmen and Their Difficulties. Mrs. Bayly. James Nisbet Co., London.

REFORMING EXISTING HOUSES BY PERSONAL INFLUENCE.

Blank Court, or Landlords and Tenants in London. Octavia Hill. *Macmillan's Magazine*, October, 1871.

Boston Tenements. Letter from Mrs. A. N. Lincoln.

Common Sense and the Dwellings of the Poor. Octavia Hill. *Nineteenth Century Magazine*, December, 1883.

Cottage Property in London. Octavia Hill. *Fortnightly Review*, November, 1866.

Homes of the London Poor. *Macmillan's Magazine*, June, 1784. Octavia Hill.

Homes of the London Poor. Octavia Hill. Published by New York State Charities Aid Association, 1875.

Open letter by Mrs. A. N. Lincoln. *Century*, 1884.

Organized Work Among the Poor. Octavia Hill. *Macmillan's Magazine*, July, 1869.

Relations of Landlord and Tenant. Miss Edith Wright. *Monthly Registrar*, March 15, 1884.

Report to Local Government Board by Miss Hill. January, 1874.

Work of Volunteers in the Organization of Charity. Miss Octavia Hill. *Macmillan's Magazine,* October, 1872.

LEGISLATION.

Artisans' and Laborers' Dwellings. Report of Select Commission, 1881–1882, Parliamentary Blue Books.

Artisans' Dwelling Bill. Octavia Hill. *Macmillan's Magazine,* June, 1874.

Charity Organization. Report on Expropriation in Glasgow. May 14, 1873, London.

Expropriation in Glasgow. Report of Sir James Watson before the Royal Institute of British Architects. April, 1879.

Homes of the Poor in London. Sir Richard Cross. *Nineteenth Century,* August, 1882.

Housing of the Poor in Towns. Anonymous. *Fortnightly Review,* October, 1883.

Housing of the Working Classes. First and Second Reports. Minutes of Evidence. Parliamentary Blue Book, 1885. London, Eyre & Spottiswoode, 1885.

Laborers' and Artisans' Dwellings. Lord Salisbury. *National Review,* November, 1883.

Laborers' and Artisans' Dwellings. J. Chamberlain. *Fortnightly Review,* December, 1883.

Laws and Ordinances Relating to Tenement and Lodging-Houses in New York. Published by the Health Department, 1891. Also by the Association for Improving the Condition of the Poor, New York. (The Philadelphia and Boston Health Departments have published similar pamphlets.)

Laws of England Relating to Tenants. W. M. Wilkinson, Esq. *London Daily News,* November 16, 1883.

Legal Obligations in Respect to Dwellings of the Poor. H. Duff. London, 1884.

Legislation sur les logements insalubres. G. Jourdain.

Logement de l'ouvrier et du pauvre. Arthur Raffalovich. Paris. Librairie Guillaumin et Cie., 1887. (Etats-Unis. Grande-Bretagne-France-Allemagne-Belgique.) (Bibliographie.)

Mischief of State Aid. Lord Shaftesbury. *Nineteenth Century,* January, 1884.

Parliamentary Blue Books, 1882–1886.

Parliamentary Return, August 10, 1883.

Rehousing of the Industrial Classes. Rev. H. Solly. 1889. London. Swan, Sonnenschein & Co.

Westgarth Prize Essays on Rehousing of the Poorer Classes. London, 1886.

BUILDING ASSOCIATIONS.

Building Associations, *American Social Science Association*, May, 1878.

Building and Loan News, 1886-1888.

Coöperative Associations—Judge Dexter. *Journal of Social Science*, 1888.

Coöperative Building Associations. Five articles, including the above. *Journal of Social Science*, 1888.

Coöperative and Loan Associations. Report by Mr. Sanborn. *Journal of Social Science*, 1890.

Englische Baugenossenschaften. Dr. E. V. Plener. Vienna, 1873.

Manual for Building and Loan Associations. C. F. Southard. *New York Star*.

Royal Commission on the Housing of the Working Classes. Evidence page 422 and Report page 43. (Coöperation in Glasgow).

Treatise on Coöperative Savings and Loan Associations. Seymour Dexter. Appleton, 1889.

WORKINGMEN'S HOMES.

IN THE SUBURBS.

Arbeiterwohnungsfrage. Trudinger.

Anlage von Arbeiterwohnungen mit einer Sammlung von plänen der besten Arbeitshäuser Englands, Frankreichs und Deutschlands, dargestelet von Rudolph Manega.

Designs for a Laborers' Cottage, published by the Society of Arts. Detailed working, drawing, plans, sections and elevations of the two prize designs. Thomas Dean. London.

Economiste pratique. Habitations ouvriers. Emile Cacheux. Paris, 1885.

Etat des habitations ouvrieres a la fin du XIX e siecle. Etude suivie d'un compte-rendu des documents relatifs aux petits logements, qui ont figuré a l'Exposition Universelle de 1889. Par Emile Cacheux. Texte et planches, Paris. Baudry, 1891.

Habitations ouvrieres en tous pays. Par E. Muller et E. Cacheux. 1879.

IN THE CITY.

Artisans and Laborers' Dwellings. Edward Spencer. London, 1881.

Better Homes for Workingmen. Alfred T. White.

Boston Coöperative Building Company. Twentieth Report. 1891.

Brooklyn Board of Health. Report, 1878.

City Residence. W. B. Tuthill. Chapter 11. The Tenement-house, seven valuable plans. New York. Wm. T. Comstock. 1890.

Documents publiés par la Commission administrative chargée de l' etude des questions relatifs a la creation des logements a bon marché pour la population ouvrière de Paris.

Devoir social et les logements d' ouvriers. G. Picot. Paris, 1885.

Grundzüge der Arbeiterwohnungsfrage. Er. Reichardt. Berlin, 1885.

Habitations ouvrieres. Rapport a la Societe d' encouragement pour l' industrie nationale, 1882.

Habitations ouvrieres en France et à l' etranger. La question des, E. Cheysson. Paris, 1886.

Haushalt der Arbeitenden Klassen. Paul Ballin.

Health in the Dwelling, etc. Articles written for and collected by the Mansion House Council. William Clowes & Son. London.

Improved Dwellings Association. Reports for 1889–90–91. Boston.

Improved Dwellings for the Laboring Classes. The Need and the Way to meet it on strictly Commercial Principles. Alfred T. White. New York. Putnam. 1879.

Impoved Industrial Dwellings Company. Reports January, 1878, and February, 1891.

Logements a bon marché dans Paris. Ch. C. More. Librairie Guillaume et Cie, Paris.

Logements d' ouvriers et le devoir des classes dirigeantes. H. Delairs. Lyons, 1886.

Logements ouvriers a Paris (Correspondant decembre, 1885; janvier, 1886).

Methods of Improving the Homes of the Poor. Stephen Smith, M. D. Paper read before the New York Public Health and Dwellings Reform Association. April, 1875.

Model Tenements. *Harper's Weekly*, January 14, 1888.

Moderne Wohnungsnoth. Signatur, Ursachen und Abhülfe. Dr. Engel. 1873. Leipzig. Duncker und Humblot.

Peabody Donation Fund. Twenty-sixth Annual Report of the Trustees. J. Grouch. 64 Queen street, Cheapside, E. C. February, 1891.

Riverside Buildings of the Improved Dwellings Company. (Brooklyn). Alfred T. White, 130 Water street, N. Y.

Single-room system. Articles by Miss Octavia Hill in *Pall Mall Gazette.* October 31, 1883.

Tenement-house Problem in New York. James C. Bayles, President of the Health Department. Transmitted to the Legislature January 16, 1888.

Tenement Houses of New York City. The Tenement-house Building Company, New York.

Workingmen's Home. B. W. Bowker. *Harper's Magazine*, April, 1887.